Signs of God
Religious Stained Glass Patterns
(35 Designs, 22 Pieces or less)

Dedicated to:

The Glory of God

and

In memory of my father Paul G. Williams

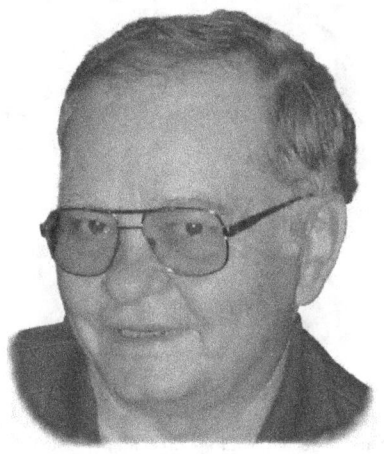

1941 - 2009

Created, Designed and Arranged by: James A. Williams

Assisted by: Cassandra Hennigan-Williams

Editor: Kelly Hoium

Signs of God
Religious Stained Glass Patterns (35 Designs, 22 Pieces or less)
All Rights Reserved.
Copyright © 2010 James A. Williams
With the help of Cassandra Hennigan-Williams and Kelly Hoium
V2.0

Outskirts Press, Inc.
http://www.outskirtspress.com

ISBN: 978-1-4327-6466-1

Outskirts Press and the "OP" logo are trademarks belonging to Outskirts Press, Inc.

PRINTED IN THE UNITED STATES OF AMERICA

Foreword

Thank you for purchasing "Signs of God: Religious Stained Glass Patterns". I have created this book for many reasons: God has blessed me with a creative mind, I have had wonderful support and lots of encouragement to push my talents further, and I haven't been able to find anything like this book anywhere in the market. Most of all, this book was created to spread and share Christianity with the world.

This book is focused on those who want to create quick religious stained glass designs and use them to spread the Signs of God.

Please send an email and share your stories with us at sogsgfeedback@gmail.com. We would love to hear from you. Please include your city and country. We would love to know how far these "Signs of God" have reached around the globe.

God Bless!

James A. Williams

Table of Contents:

Introduction

Here are some of the features of this book:

- The patterns require no more than 22 pieces of glass per panel.

- The designs in this book were created to be used with the copper foil method of stained glass design and are simple enough for those with beginner / intermediate skill levels.

- Each of the designs uses fairly simple shapes and can be created, on average, in 2 weeks or less. The designs were created to be enlarged to and constructed at a size of 11 x 14 inches.

- All patterns feature some symbol, figure, story or act dealing with Christianity.

- Every design in this book is an original design created by James Williams.

- There are a few designs that have overlays and/or bevels:

    o Overlays are denoted by a straight or curved dotted line like this: - - - - - -

    o Bevels are denoted by the following graphic:

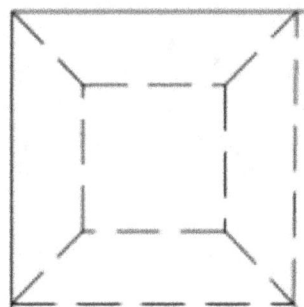

(If you do not have a bevel you can always use a regular piece of glass of your choice instead.)

…And now, the designs! Have fun!

#1 INRI

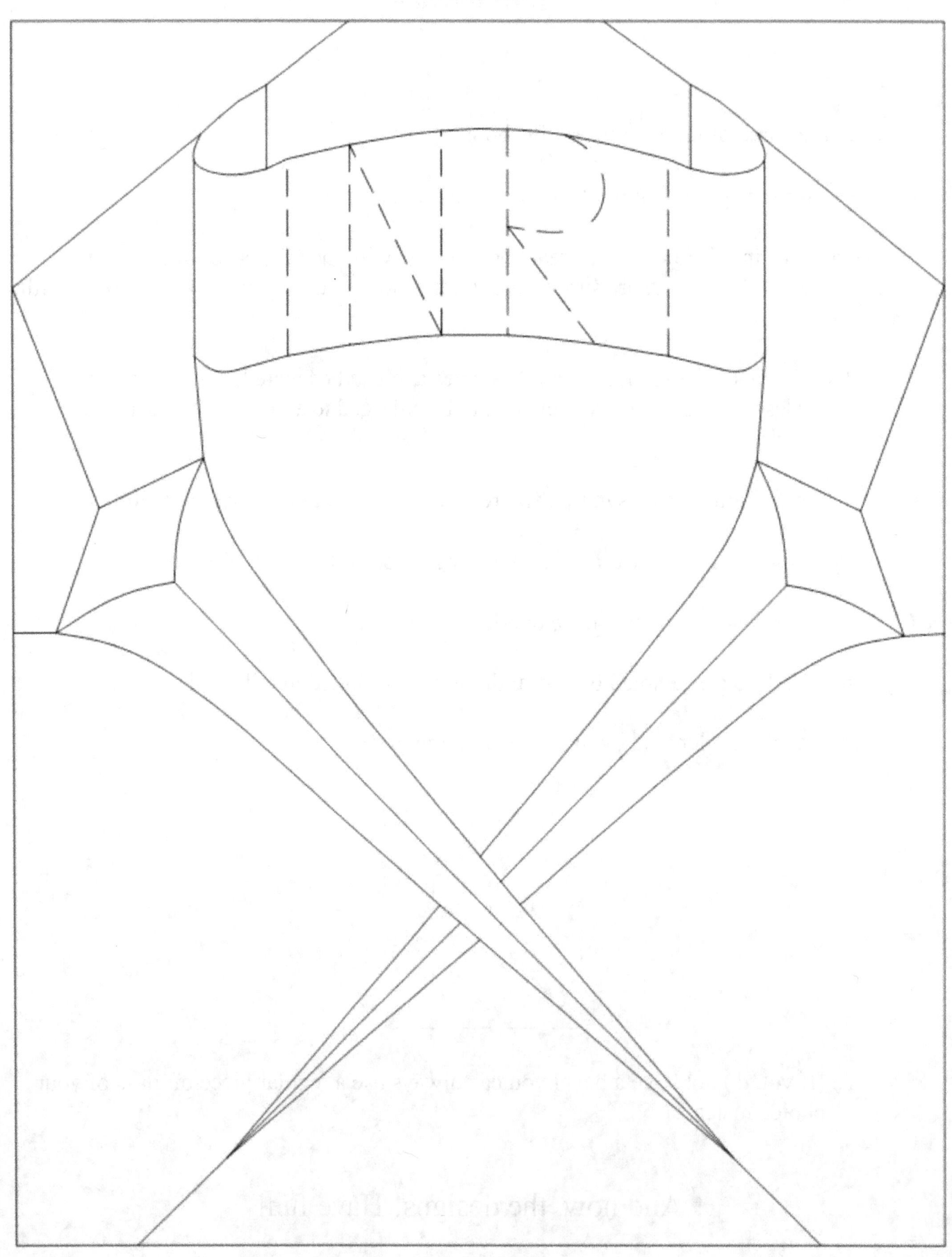

#2 Easter Lily

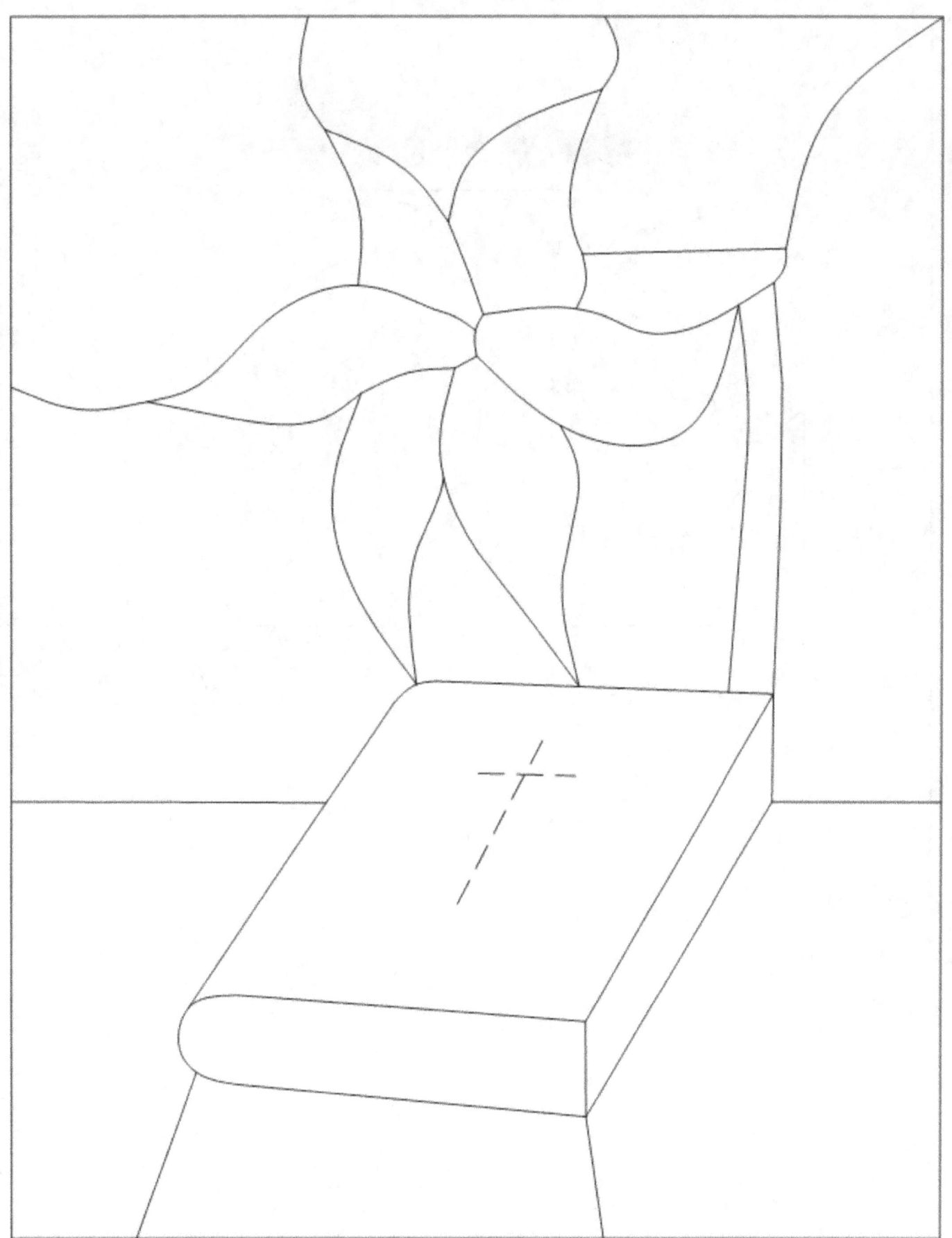

#3 Celtic Cross

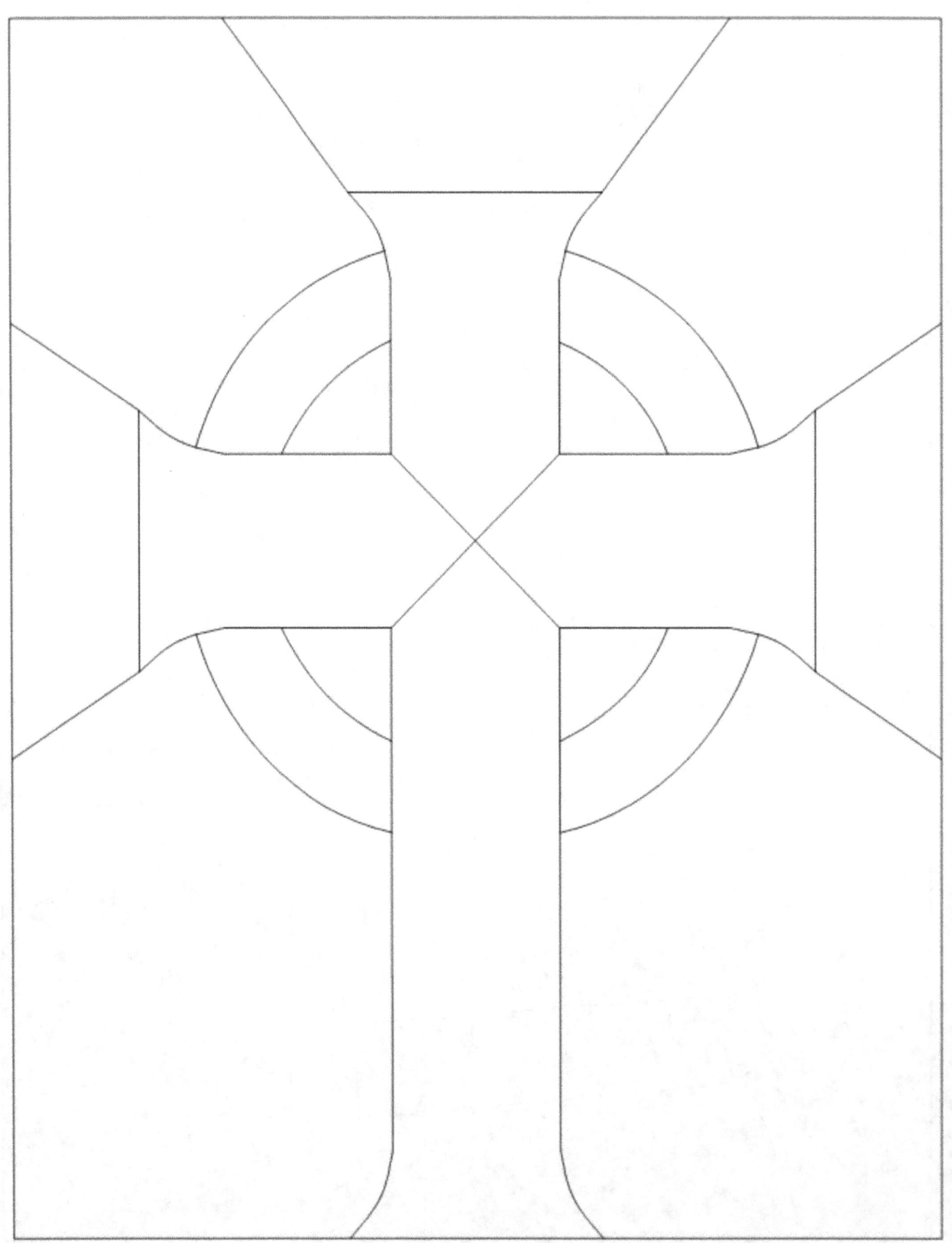

#4 Eucharist and Wine

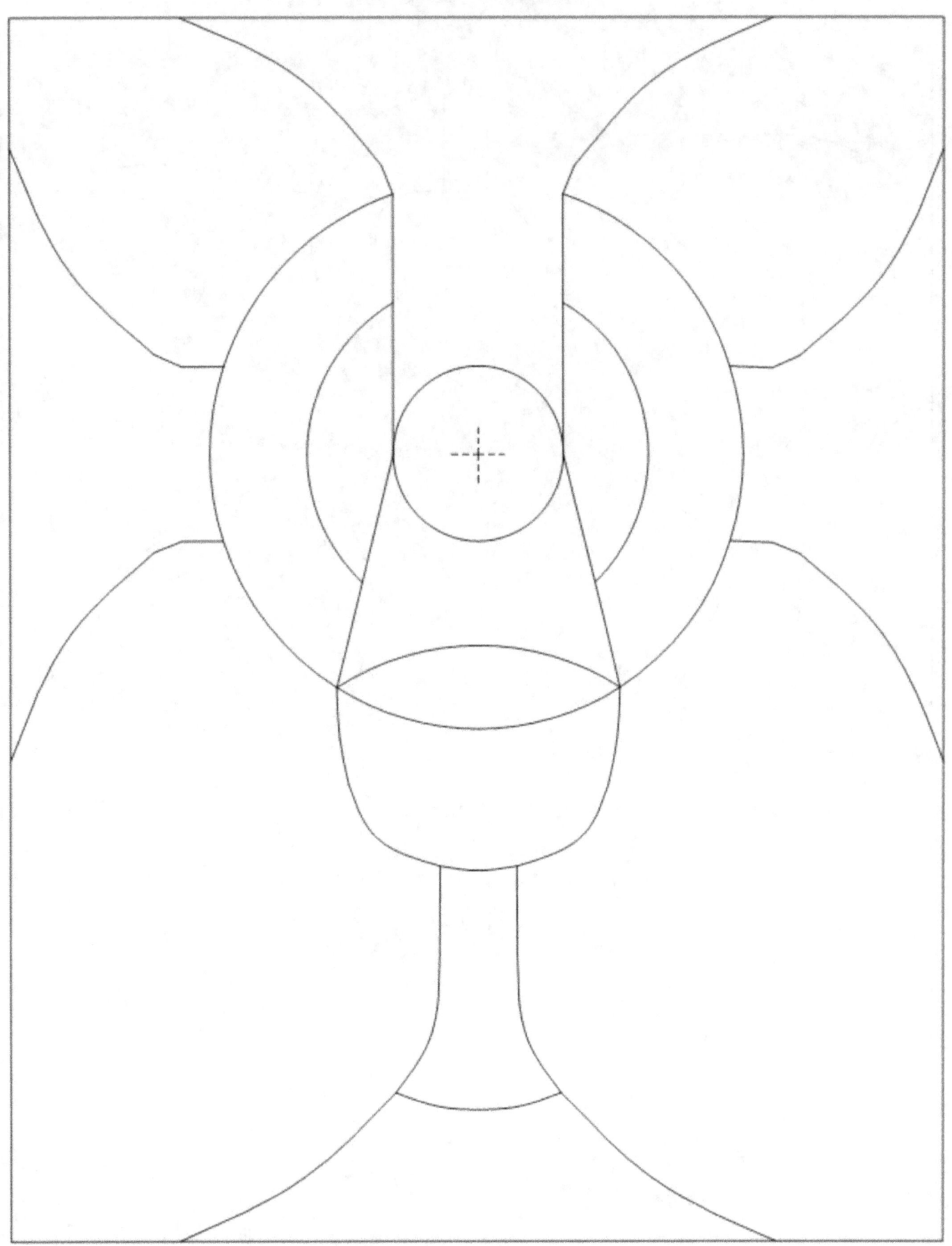

#5 Angel

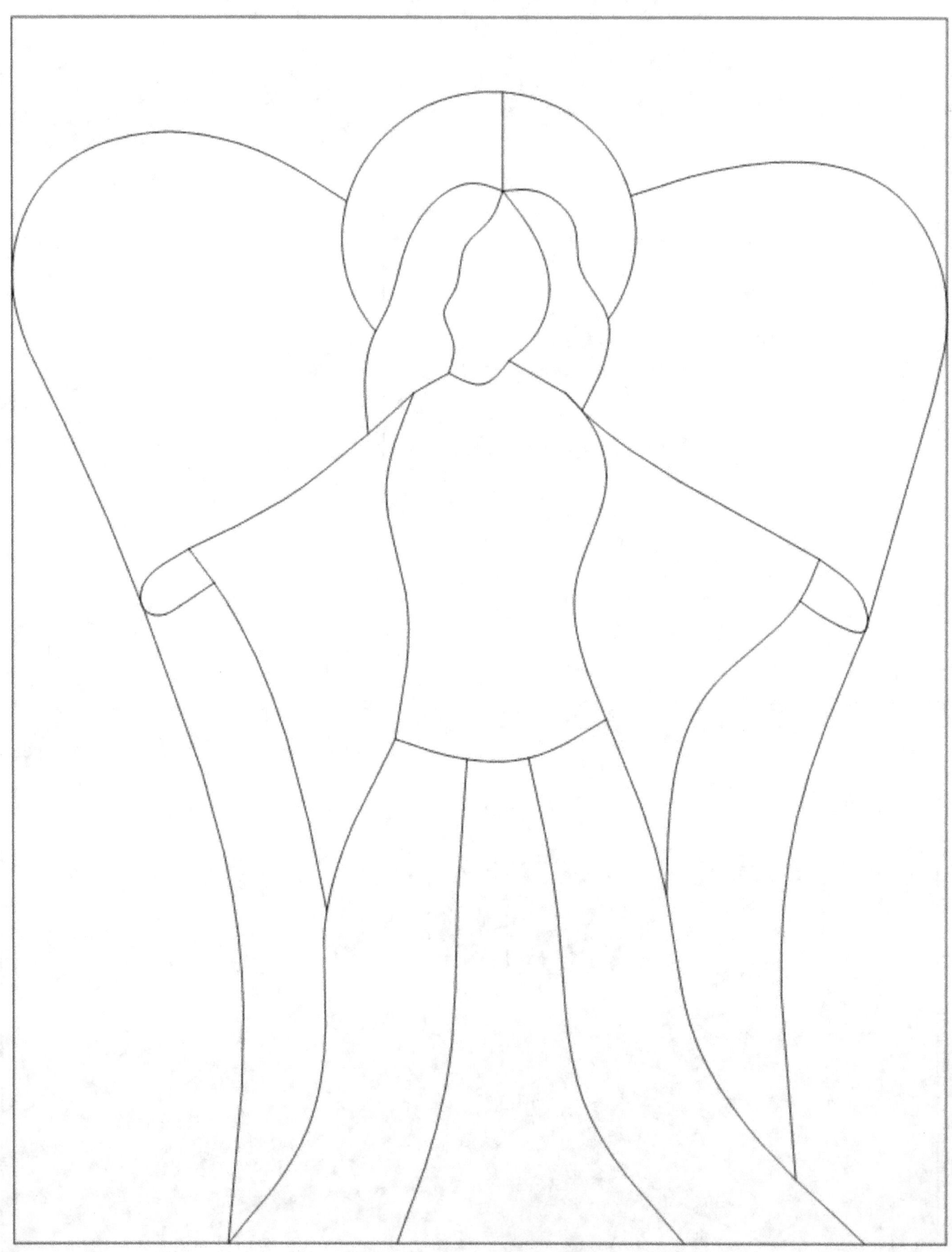

#6 Dove of Peace (Holy Spirit) - (NOTE: Eye of dove is an overlay)

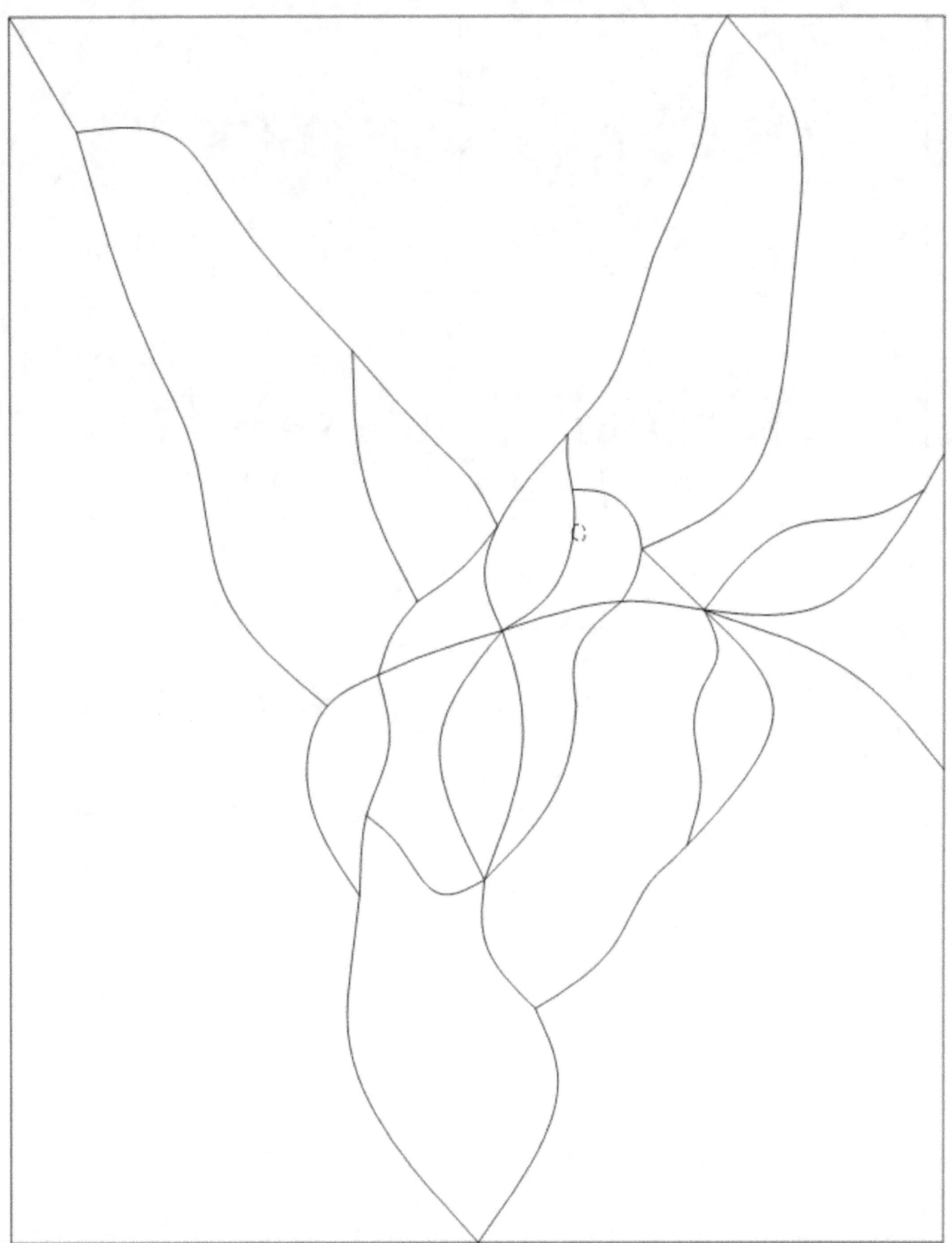

#7 Christian Fish (Ichthus)

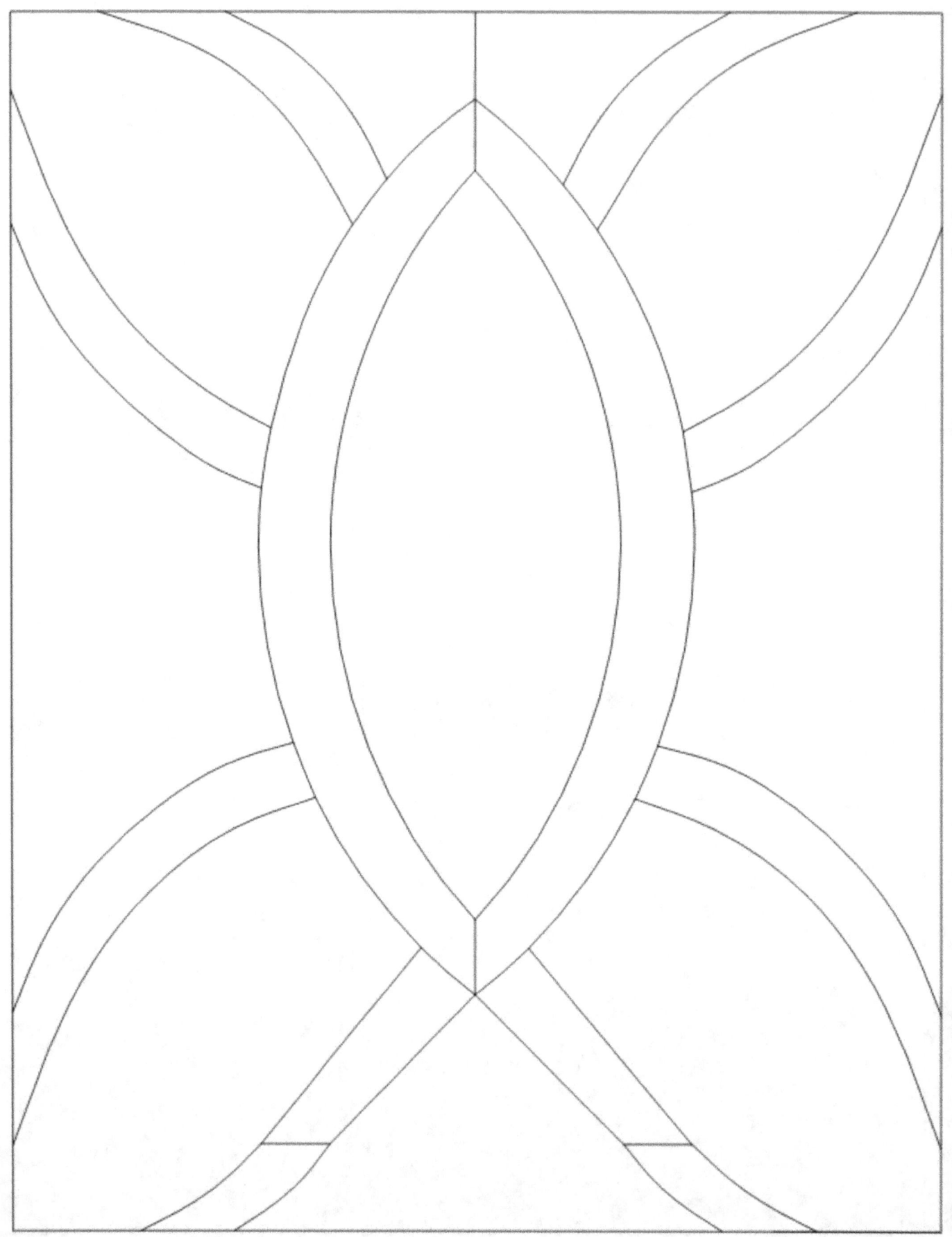

#8 Cross with Rings (Marriage)

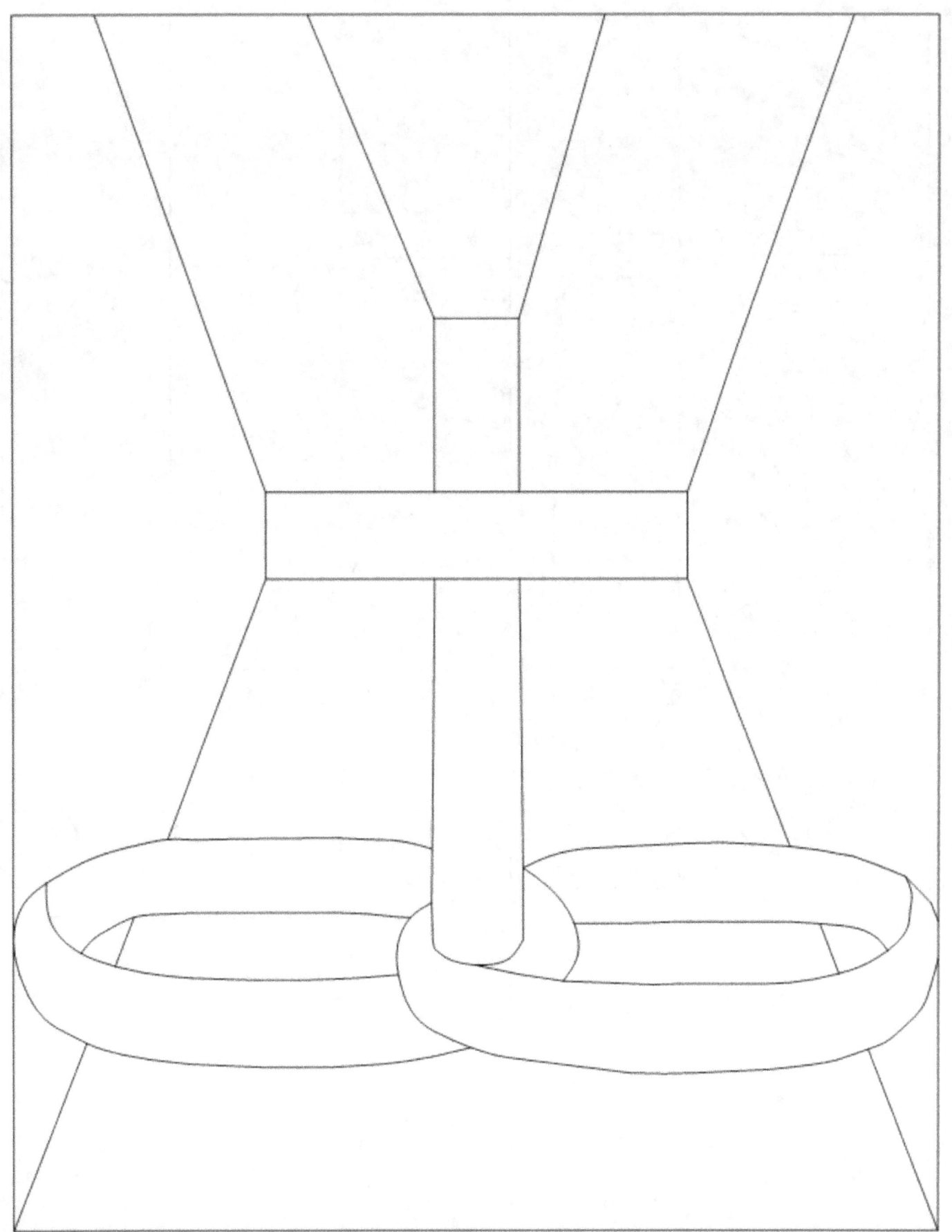

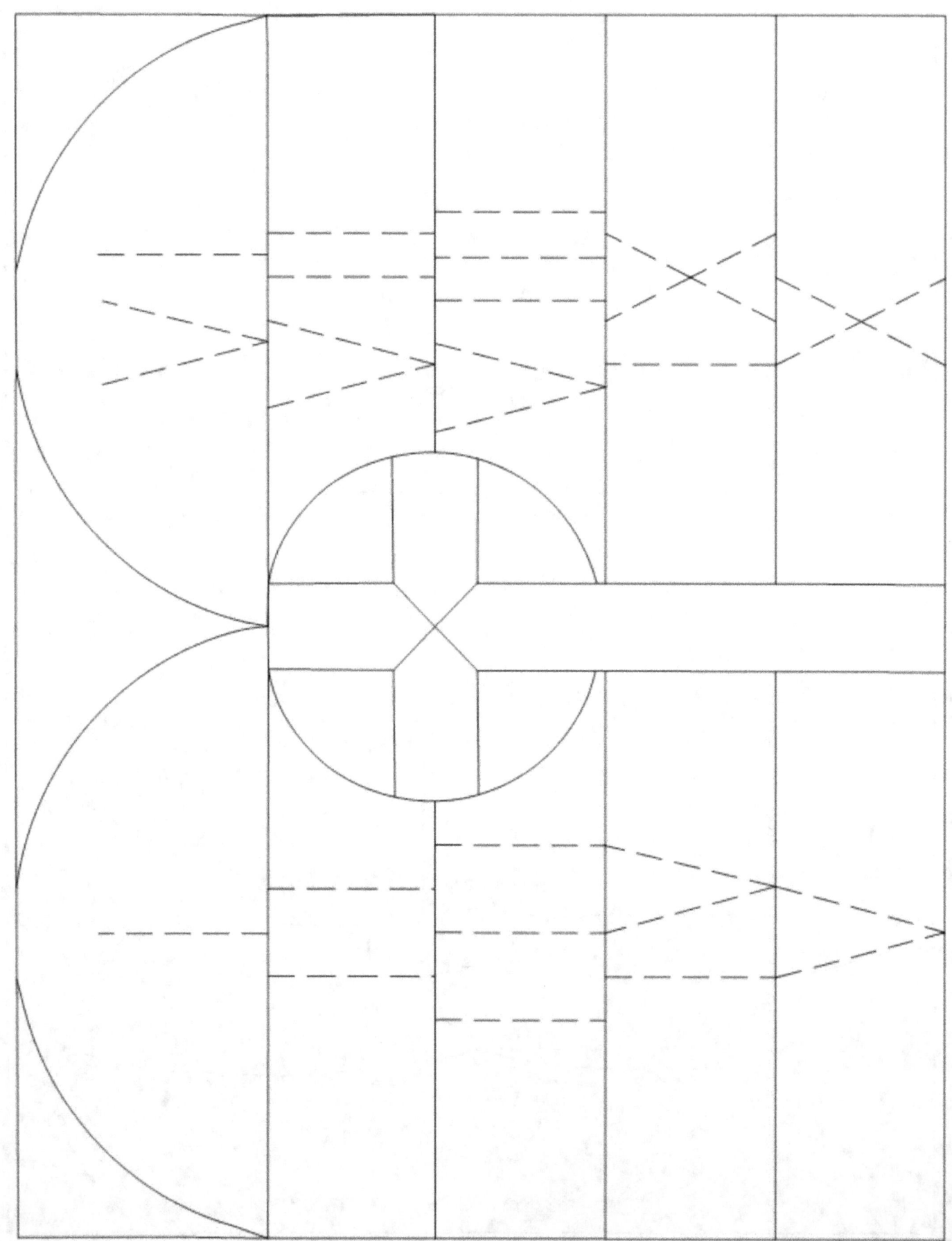

#10 Bread and Wine (NOTE: Indents on bread are overlays.)

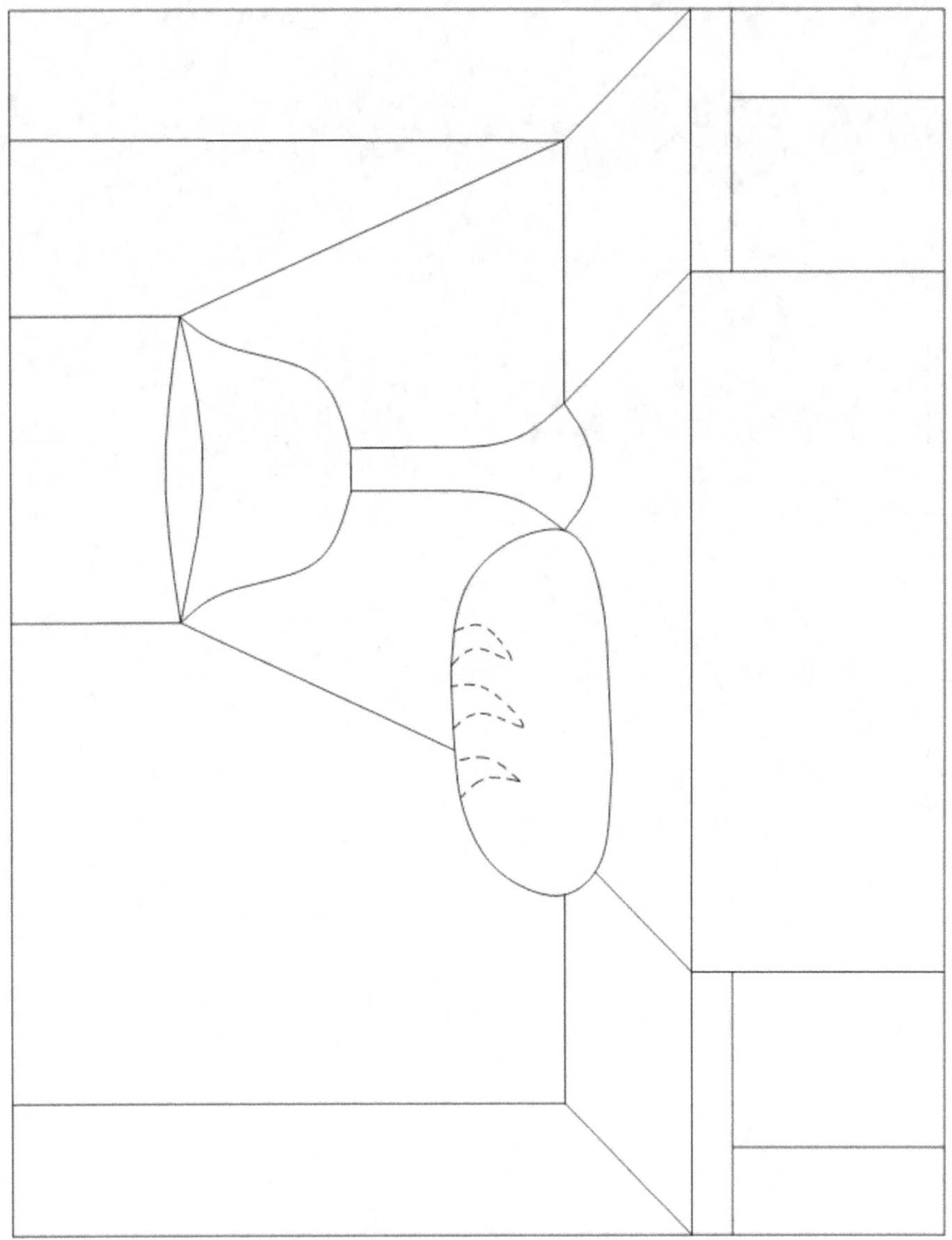

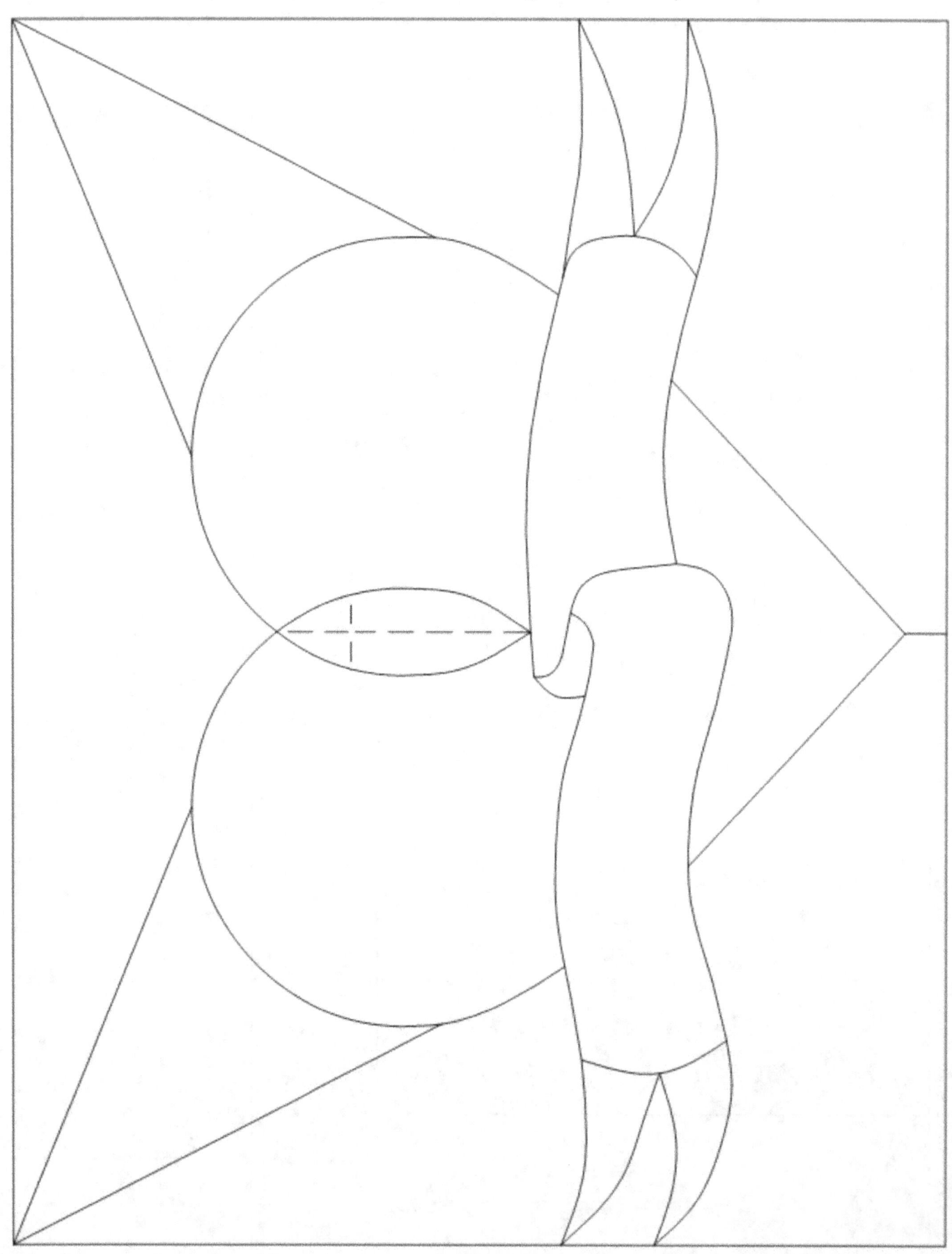

#12 Alpha and Omega

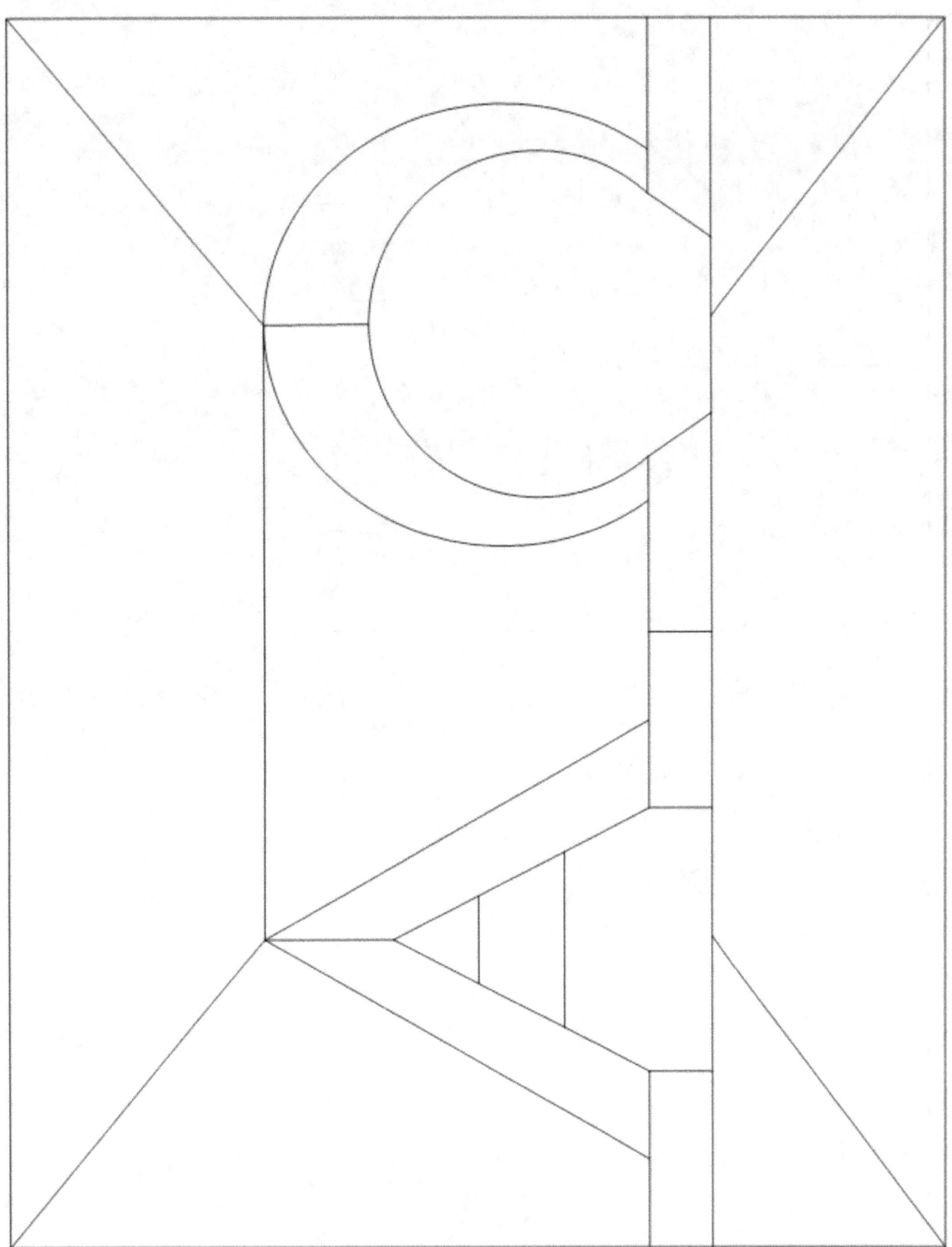

#13 Prism Cross

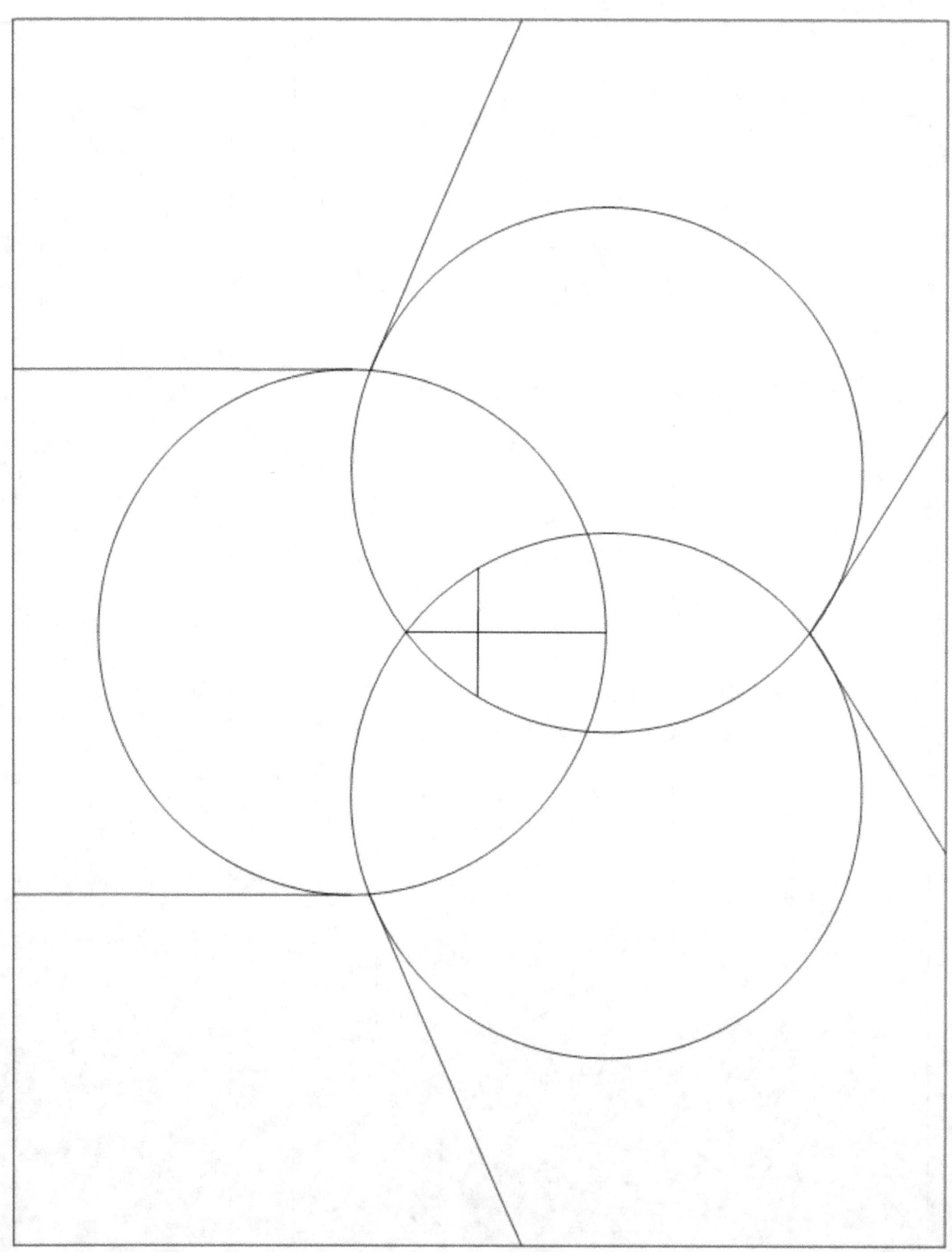

#14 The World in His Hands

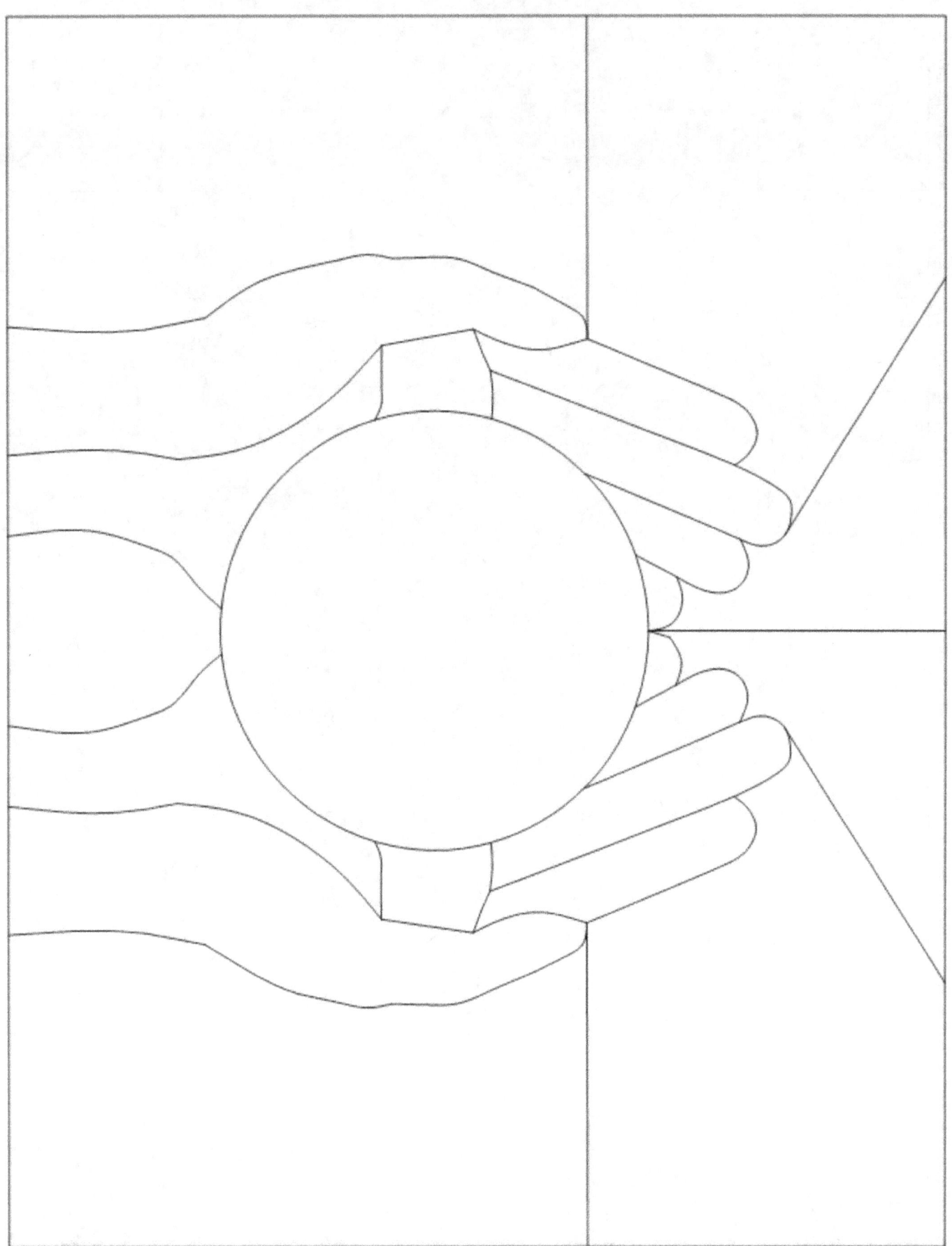

#15 Mary and Jesus

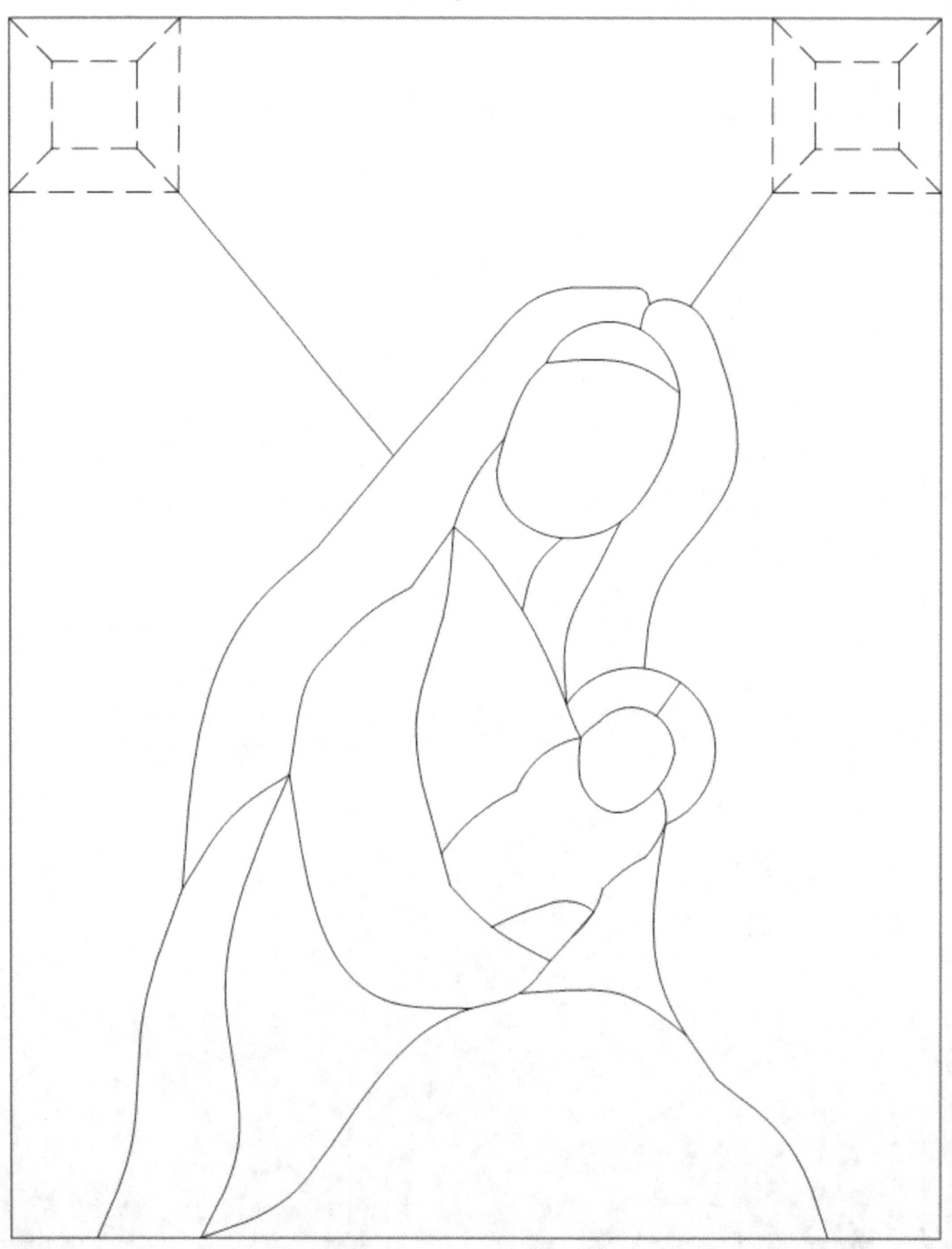

#16 Chi Rho

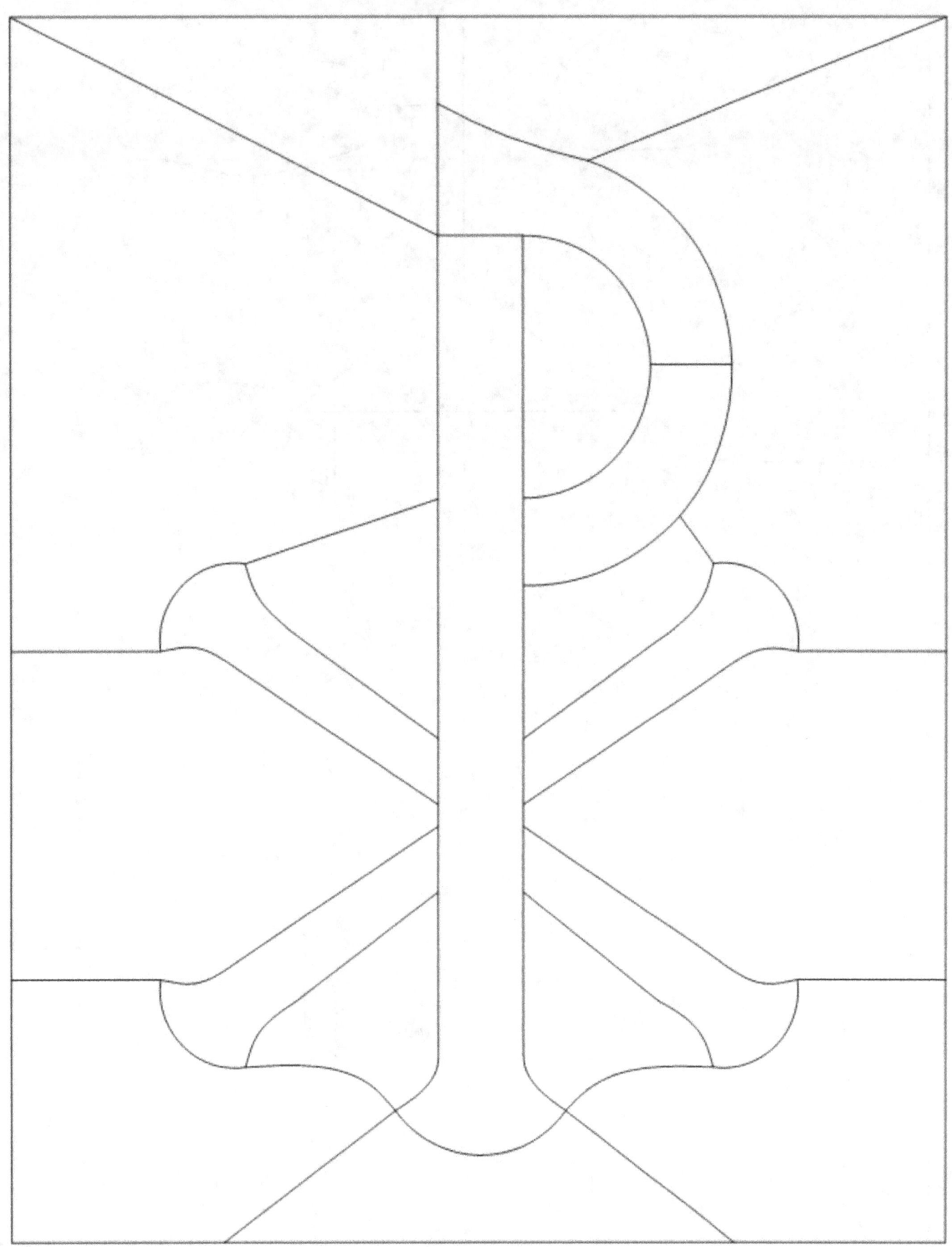

#17 Church

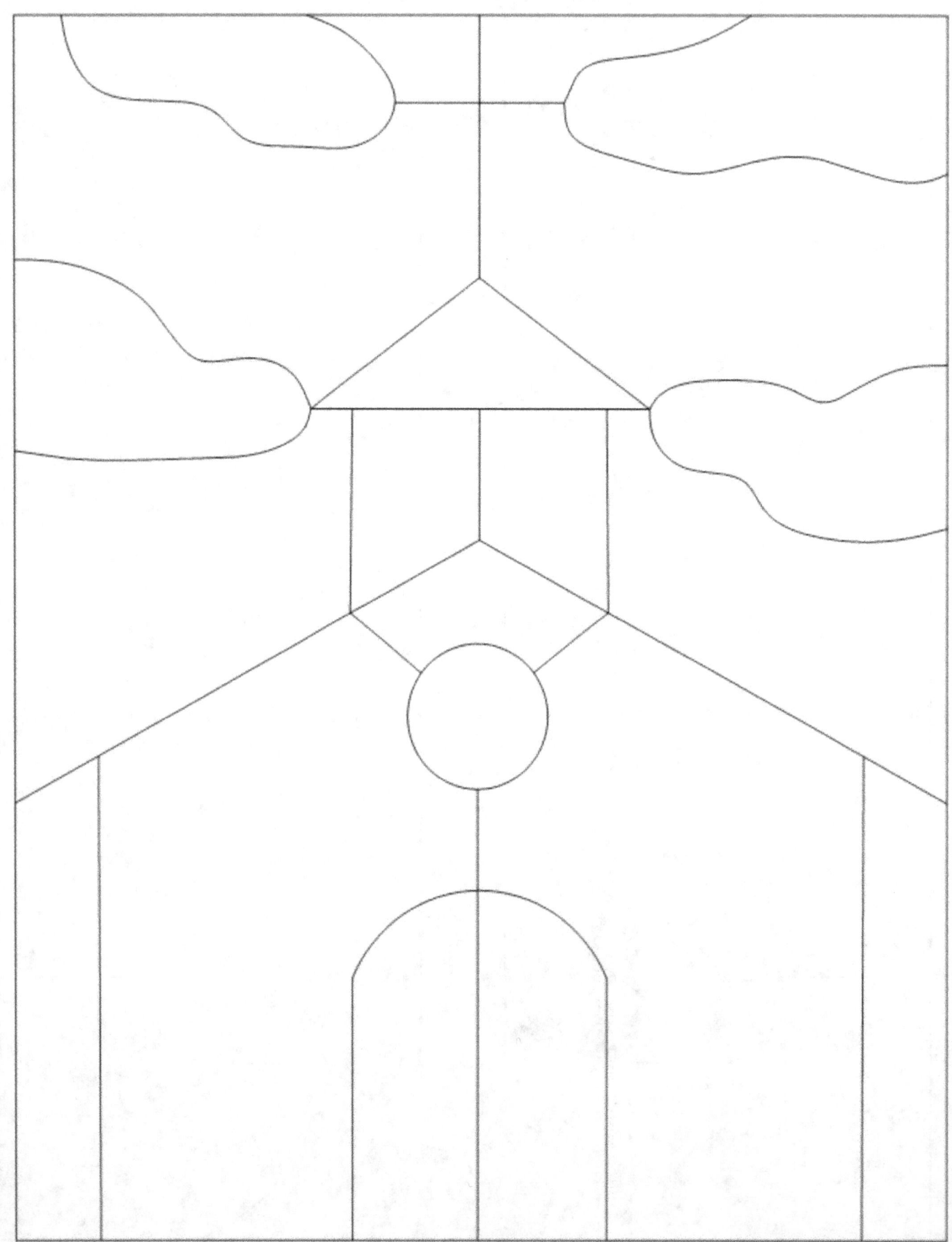

#18 Burning Bush

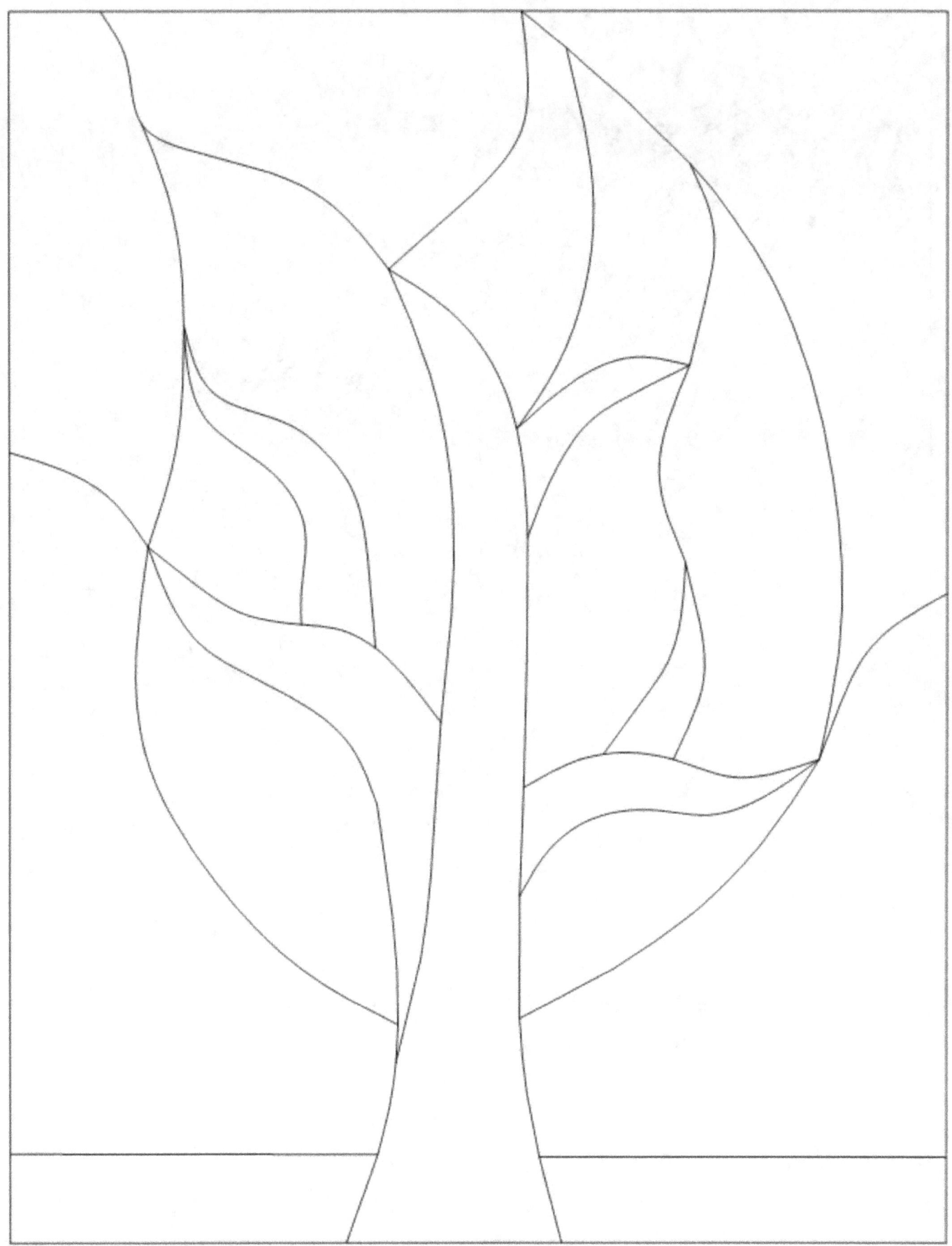

#19 Moses and the Ten Commandments

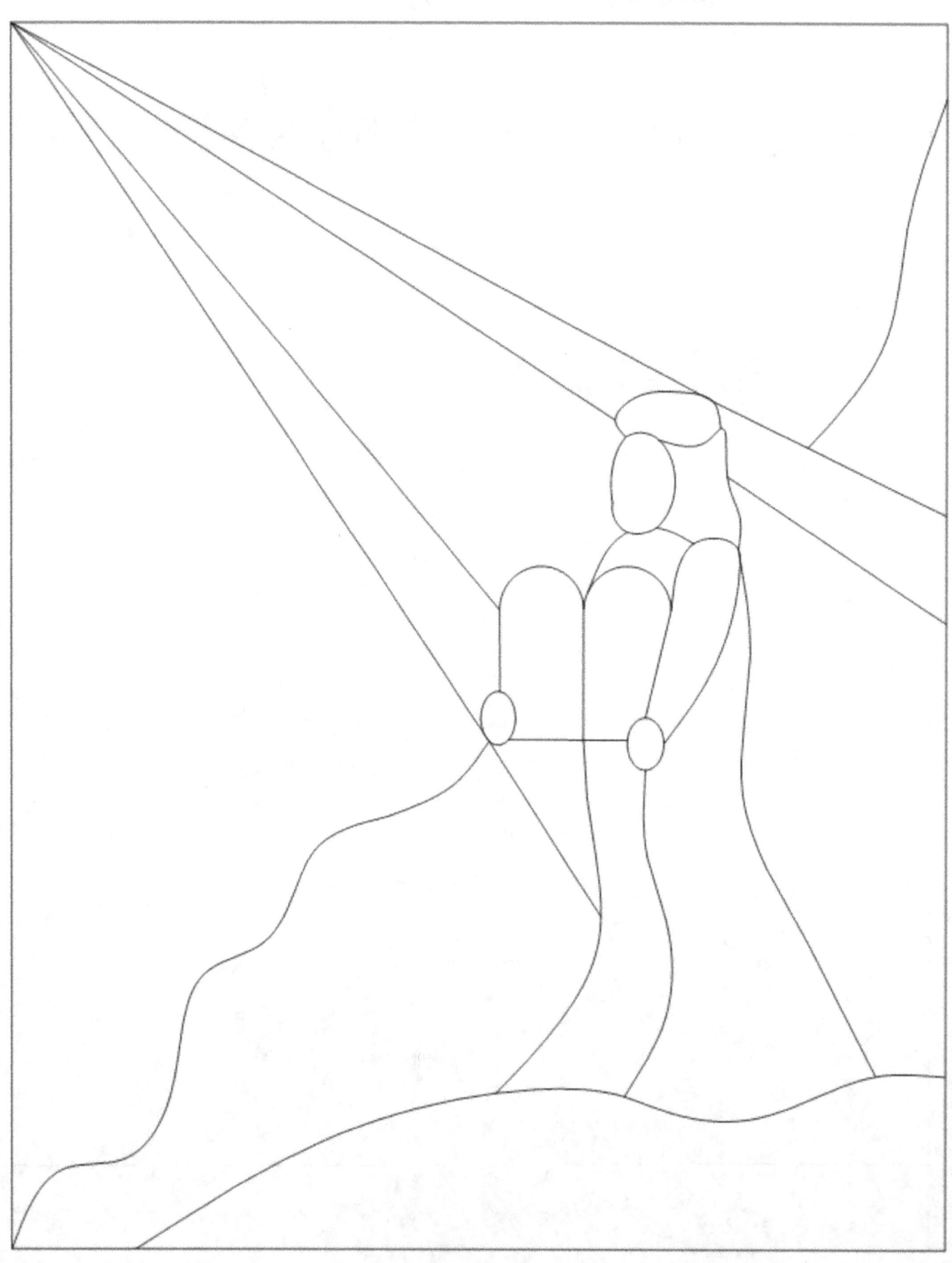

#20 Shepherd

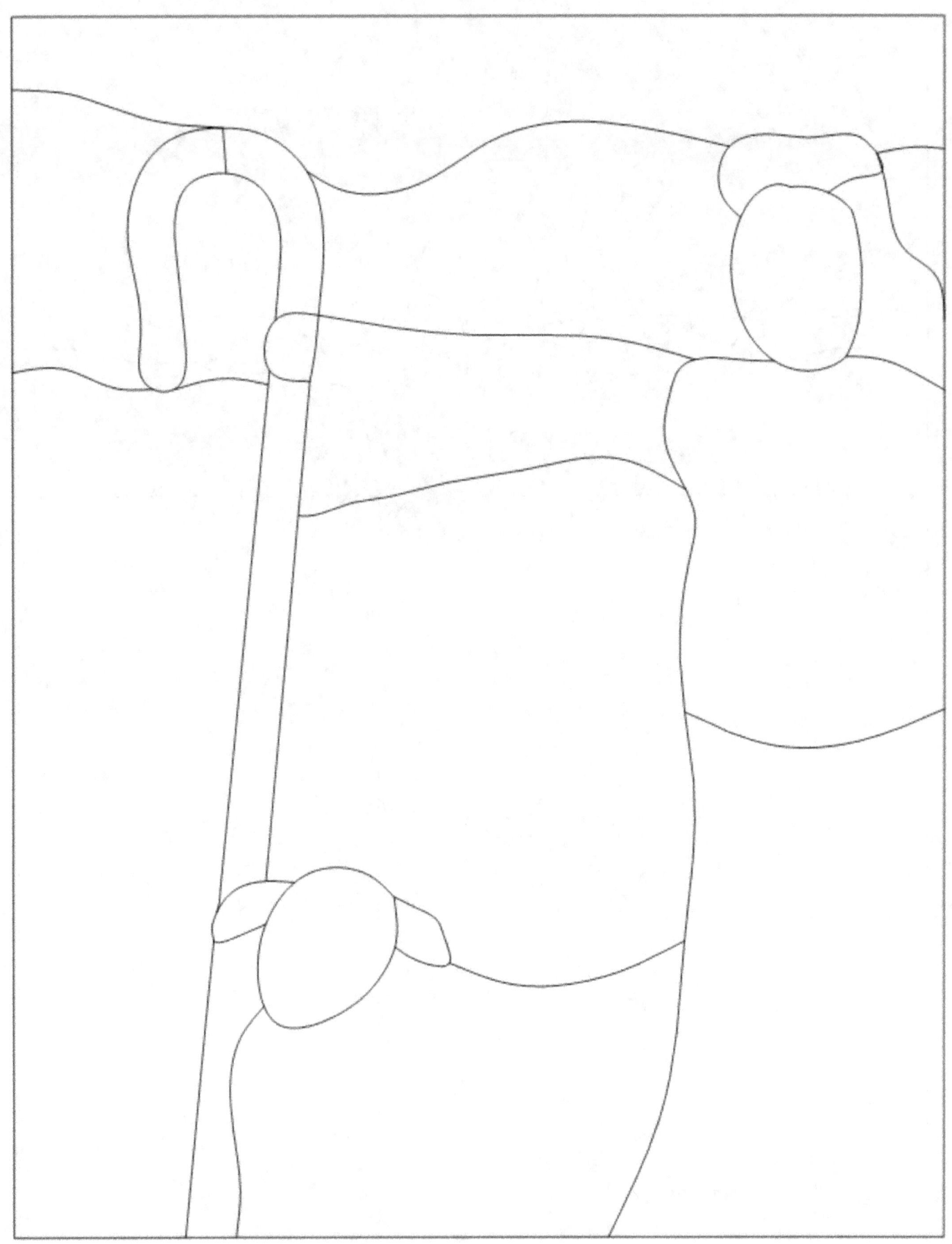

#21 Crucifixion

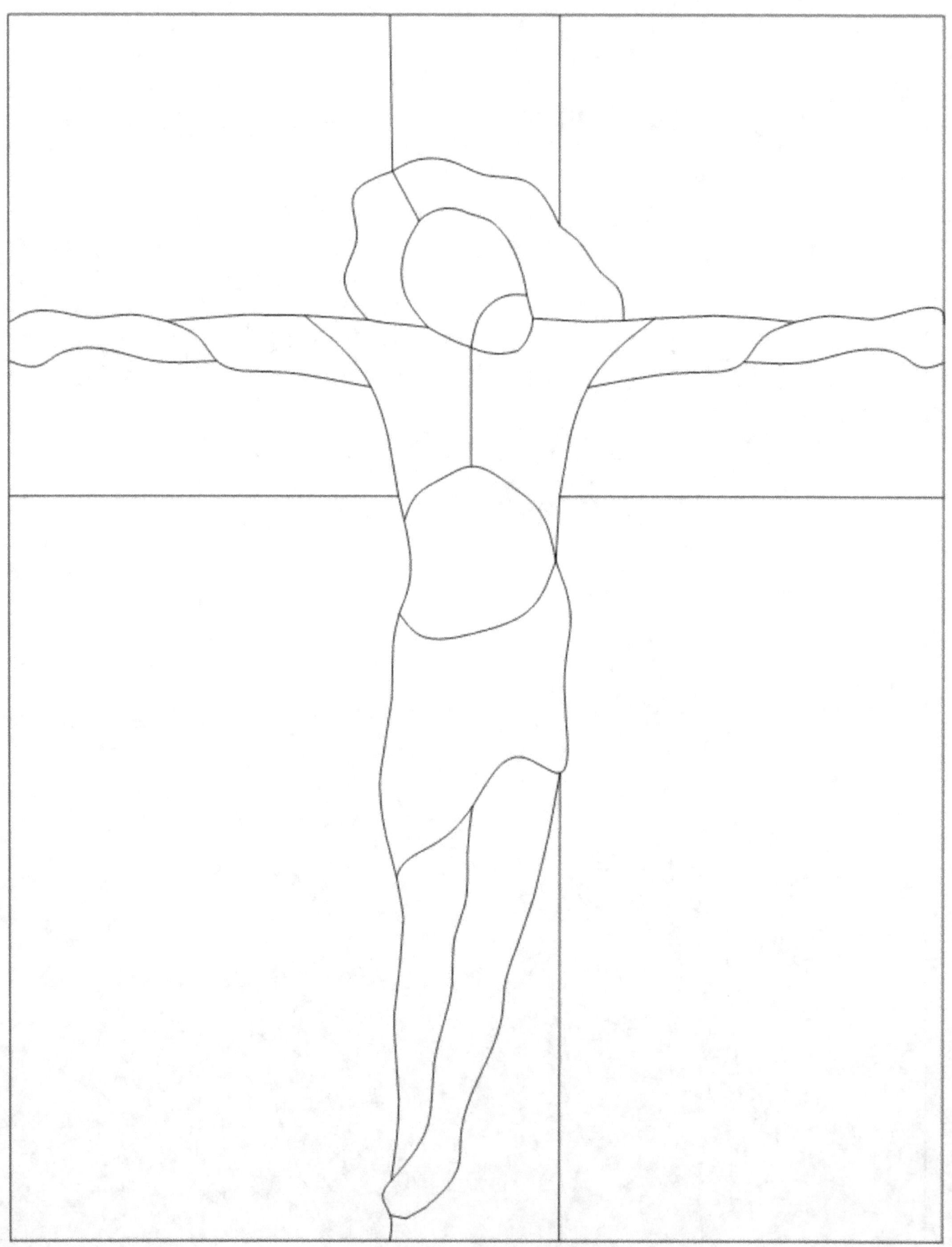

#22 Jesus Walking on the Water

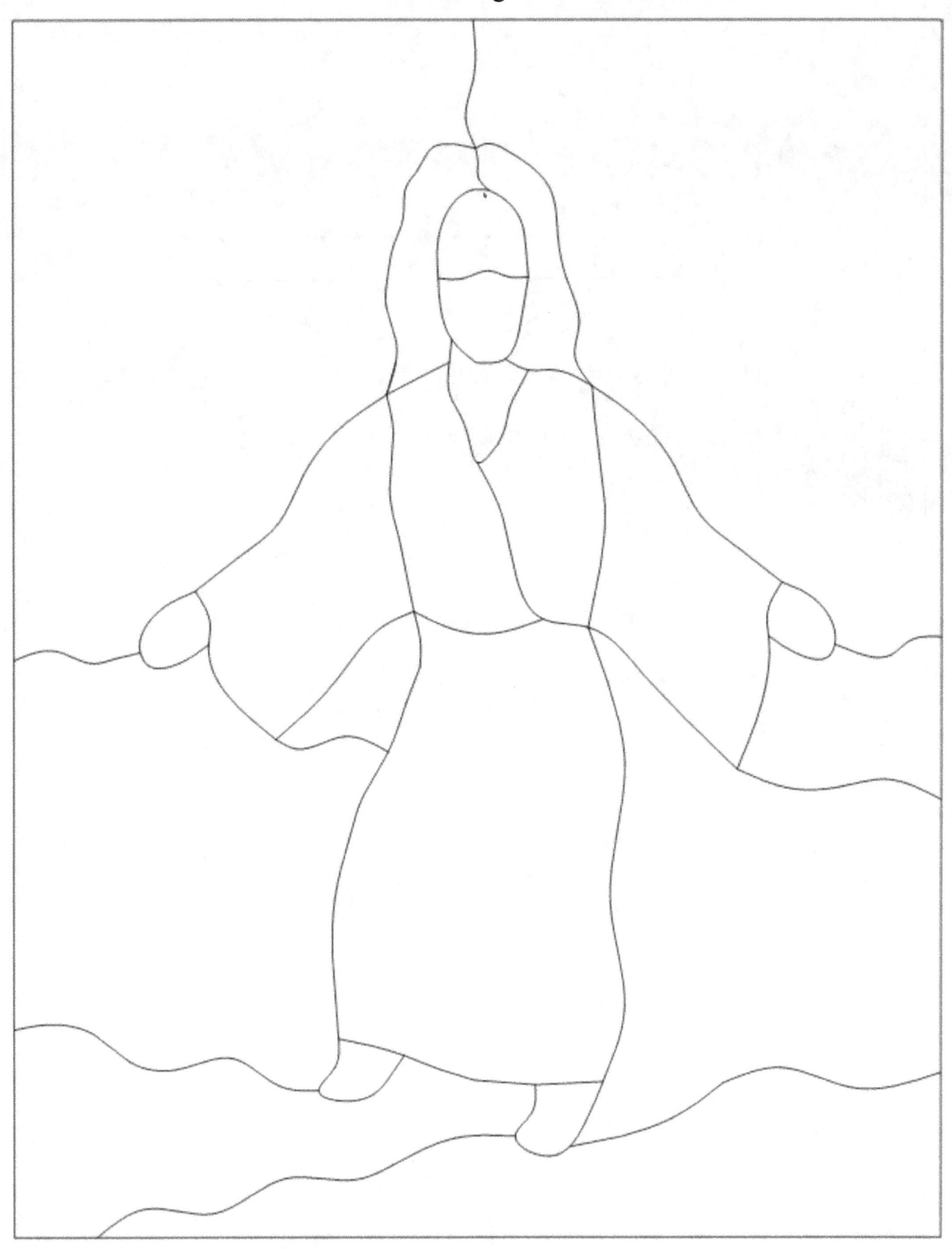

#22 Jesus Walking on the Water

#23 Moses Parts the Sea

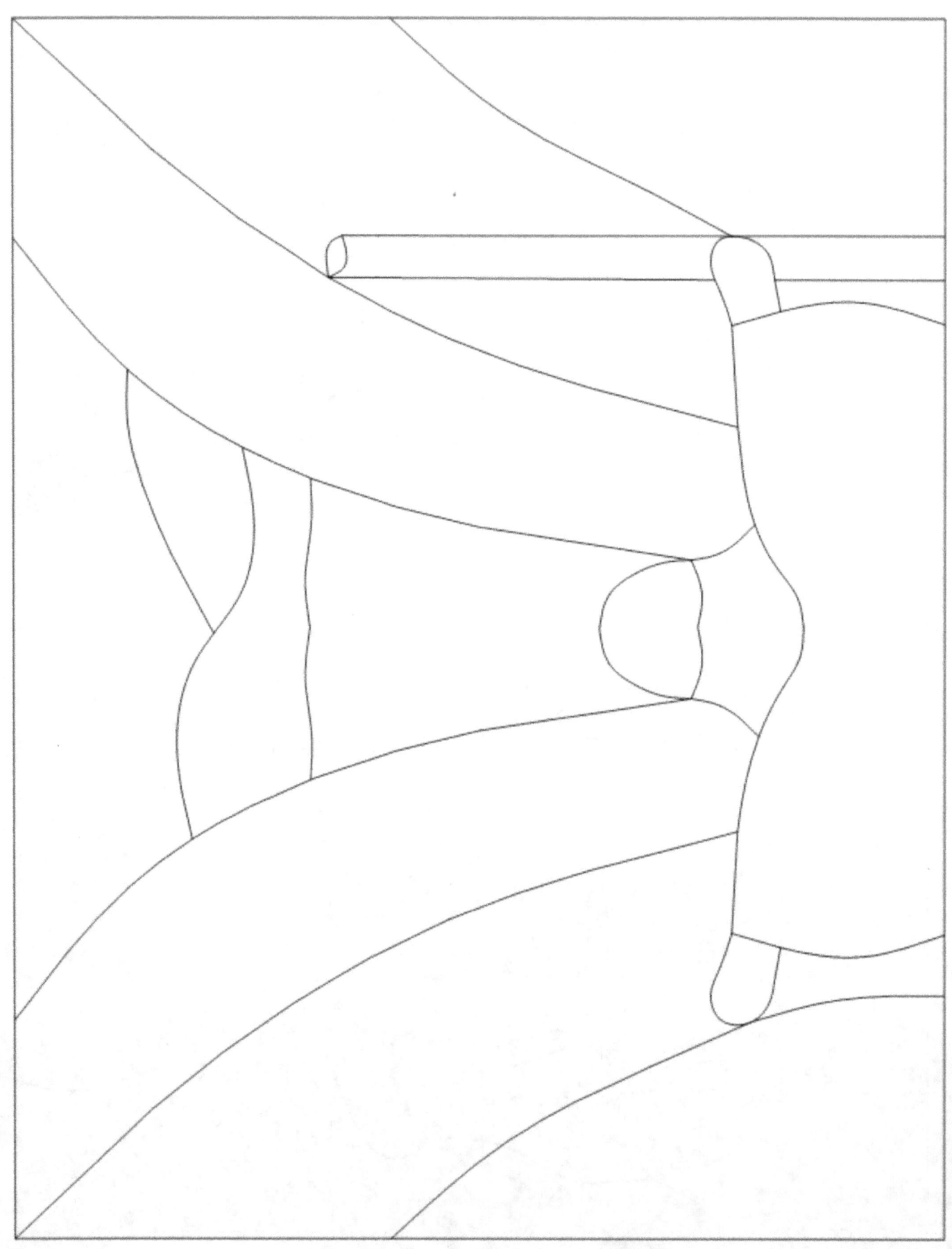

#23 Moses Parts the Sea

#24 Noah's Ark

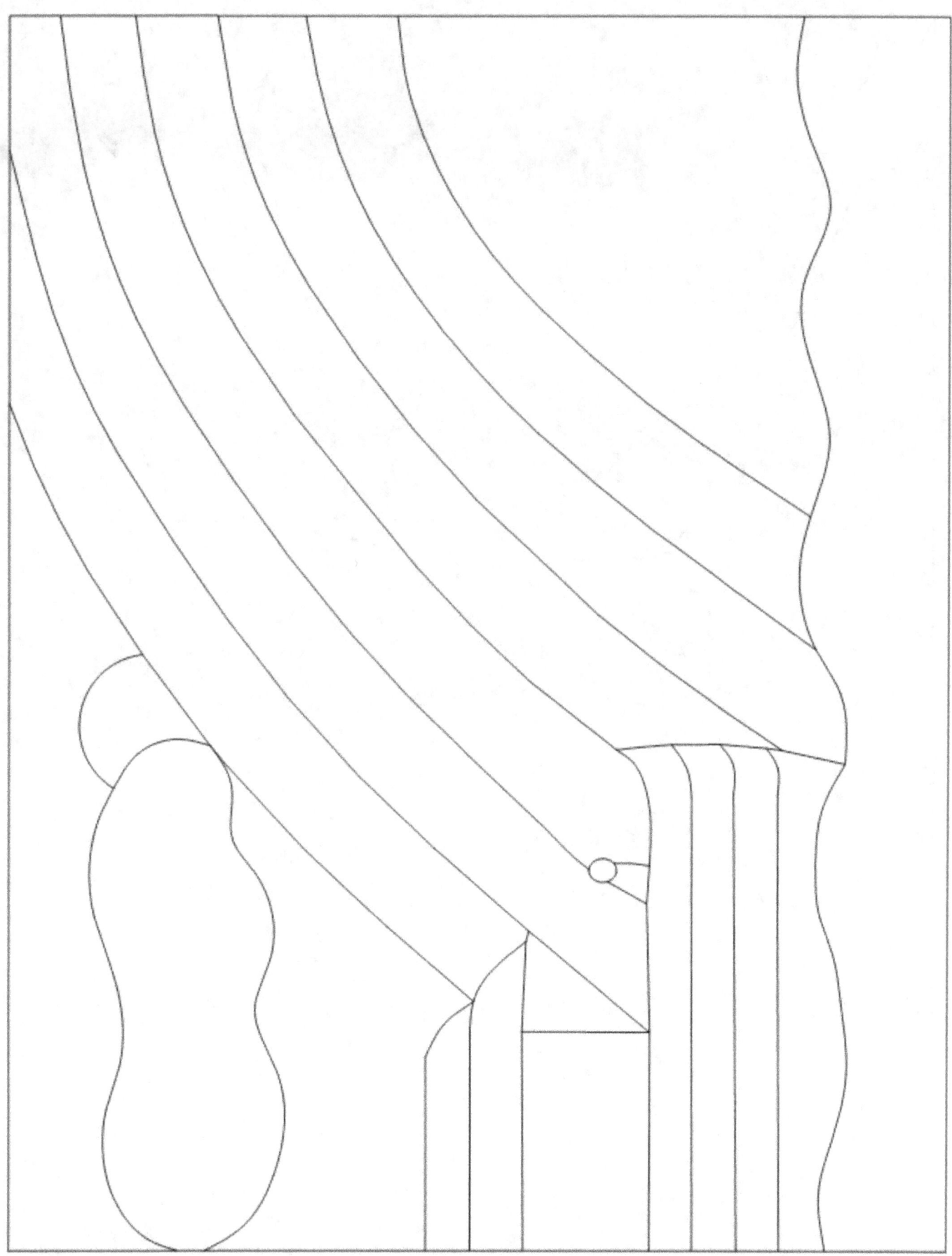

#25 Resurrection

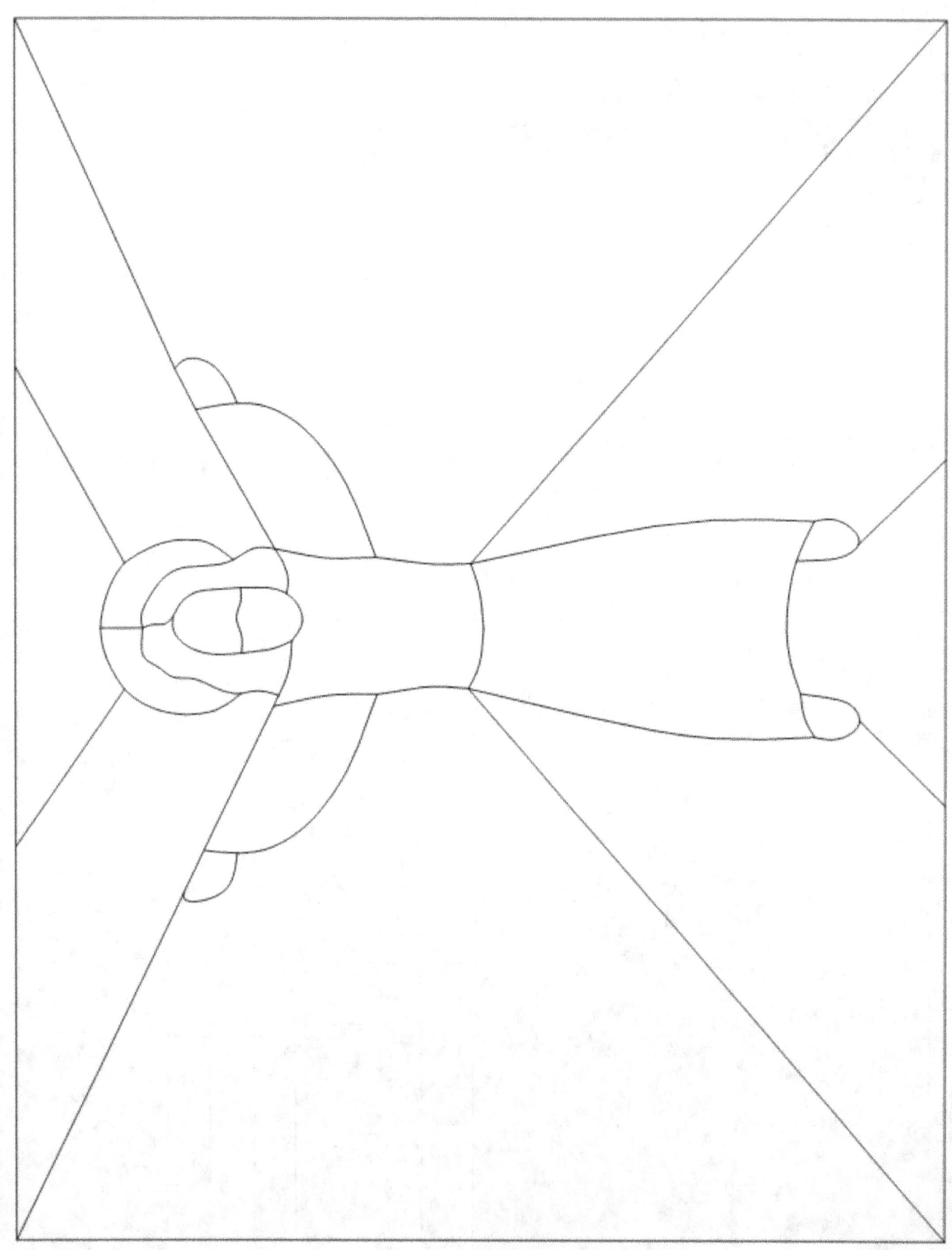

#26 Baptism

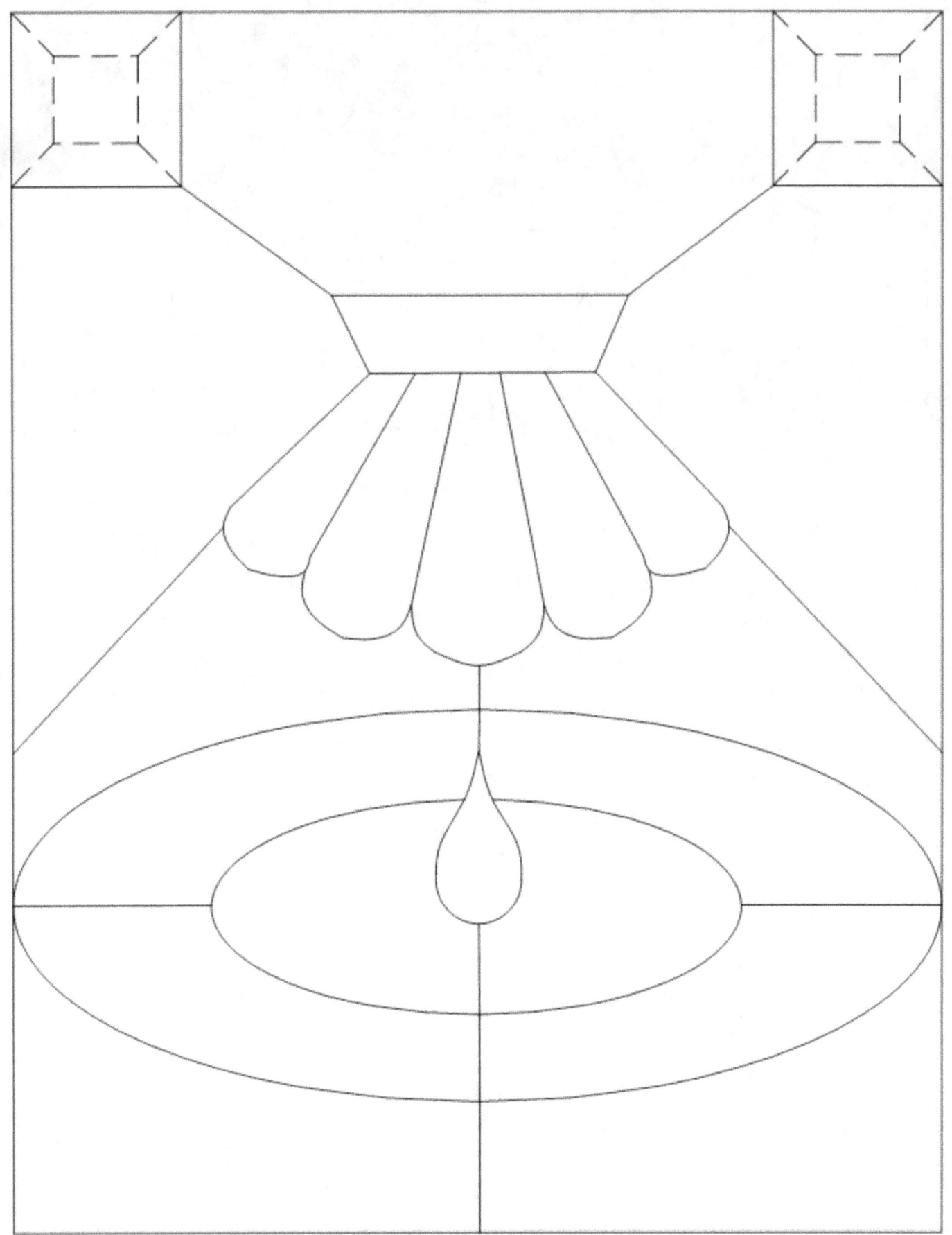

#27 Garden of Eden

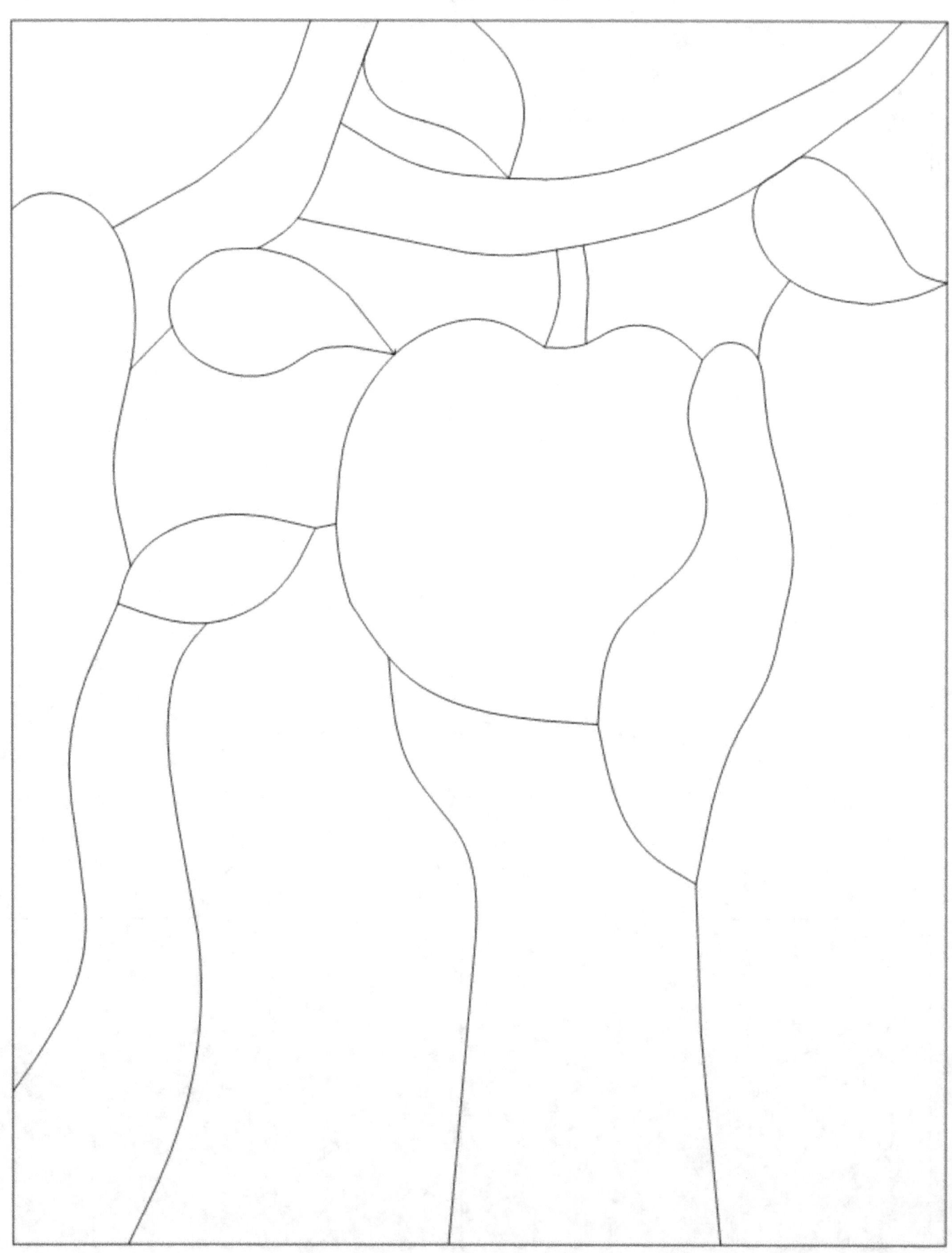

#28 Nativity (Holy Family)

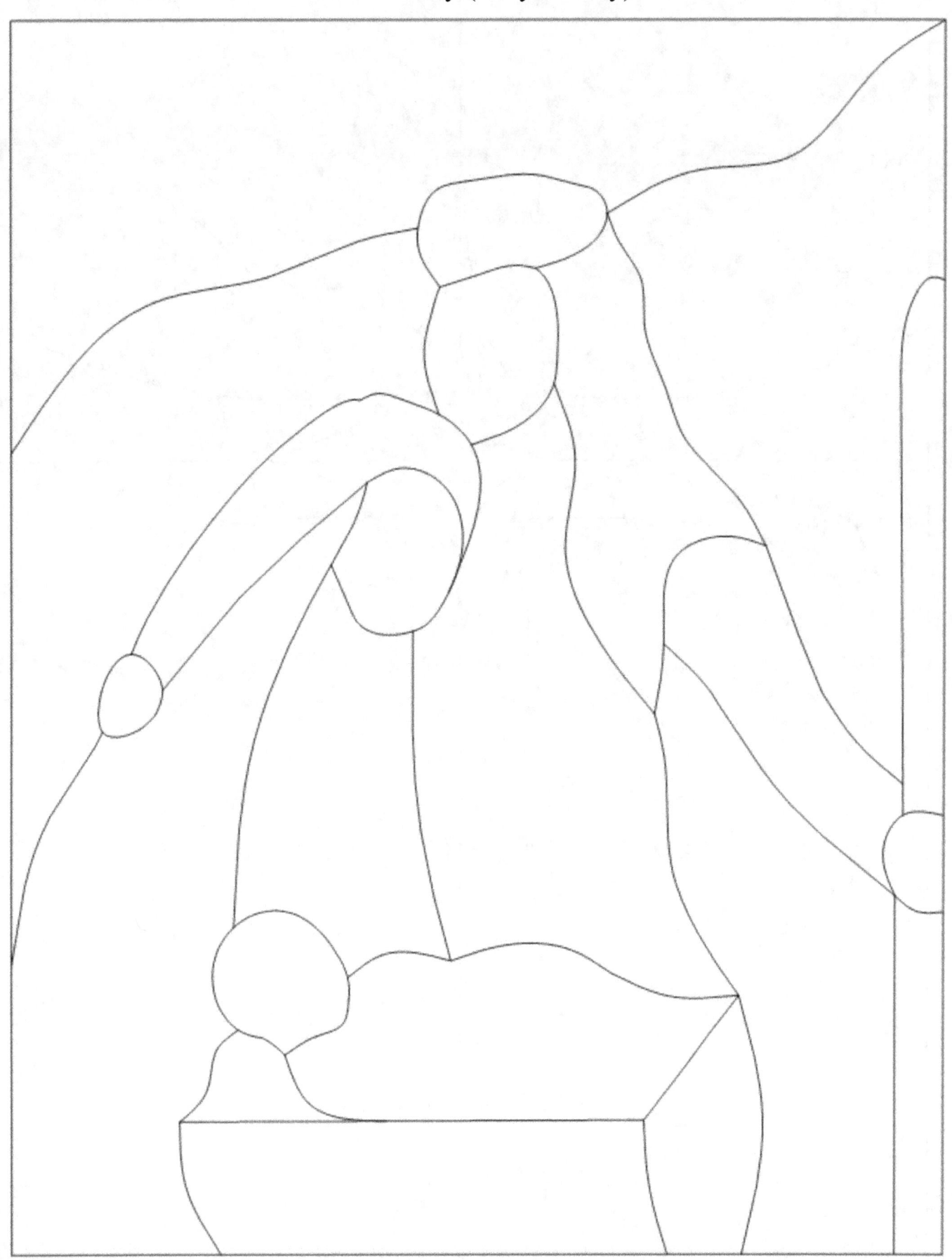

#29 Star of Bethlehem Cross

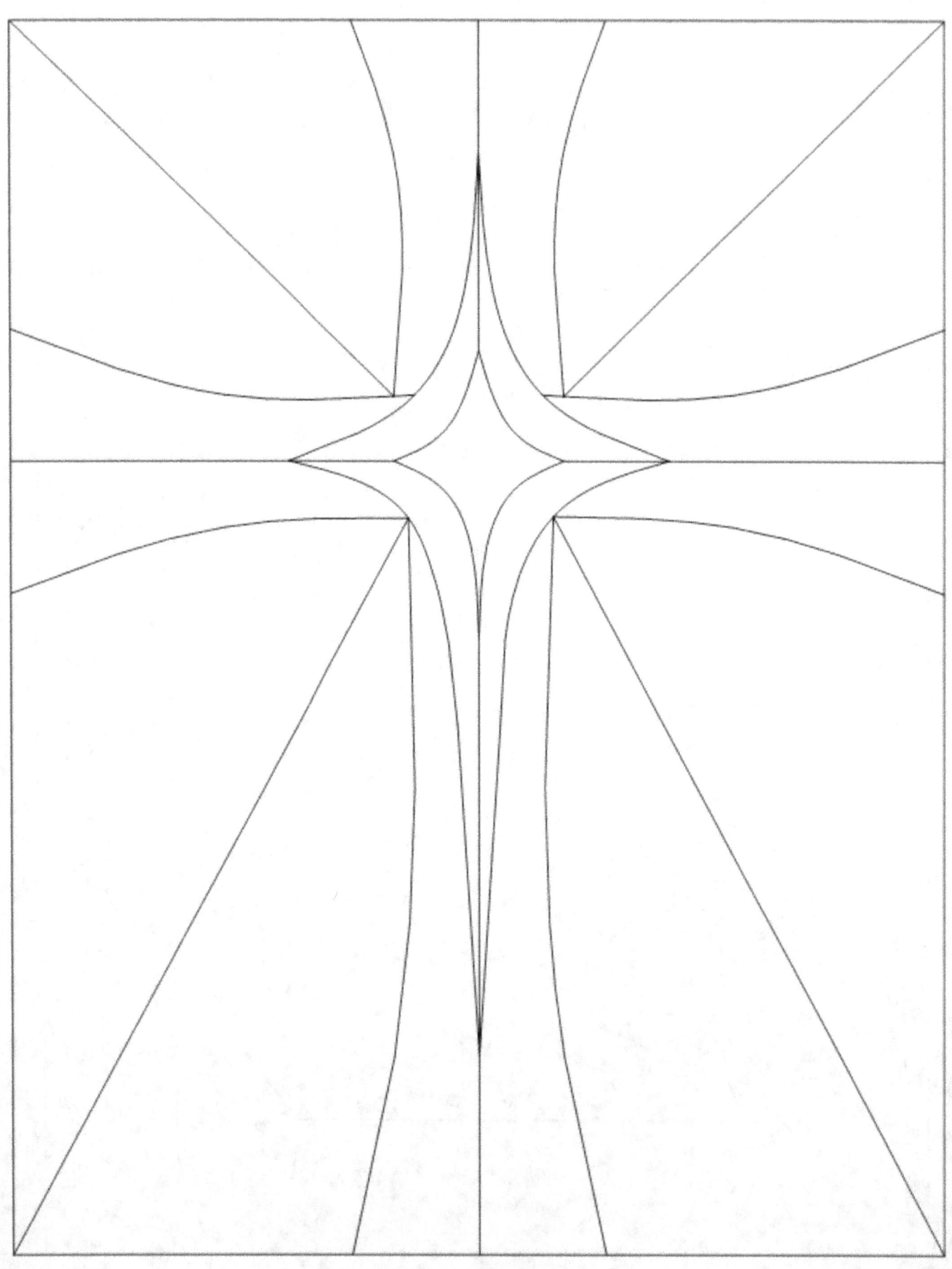

#30 Choir (NOTE: All notes and mouth are overlays)

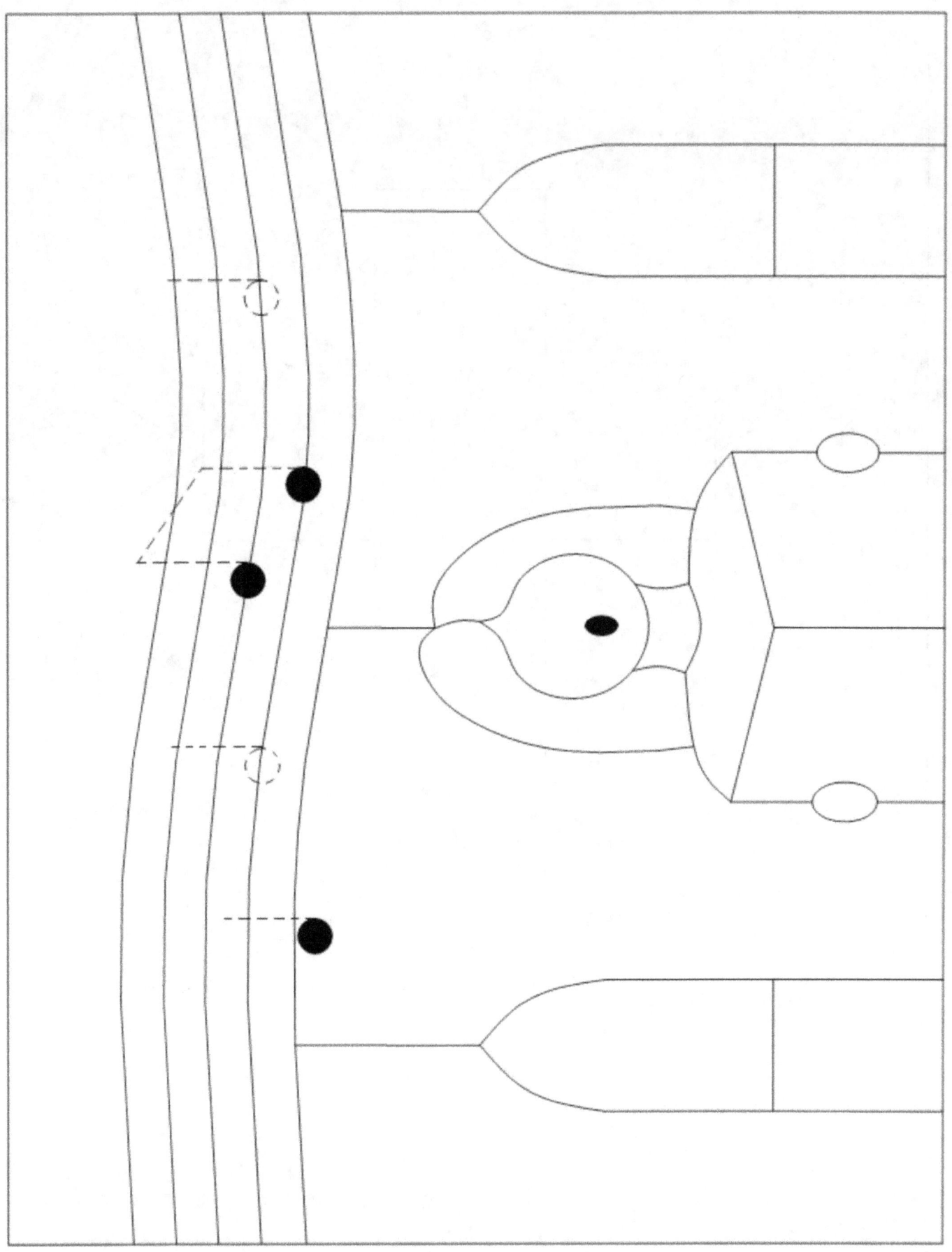

#31 Cross and Stream

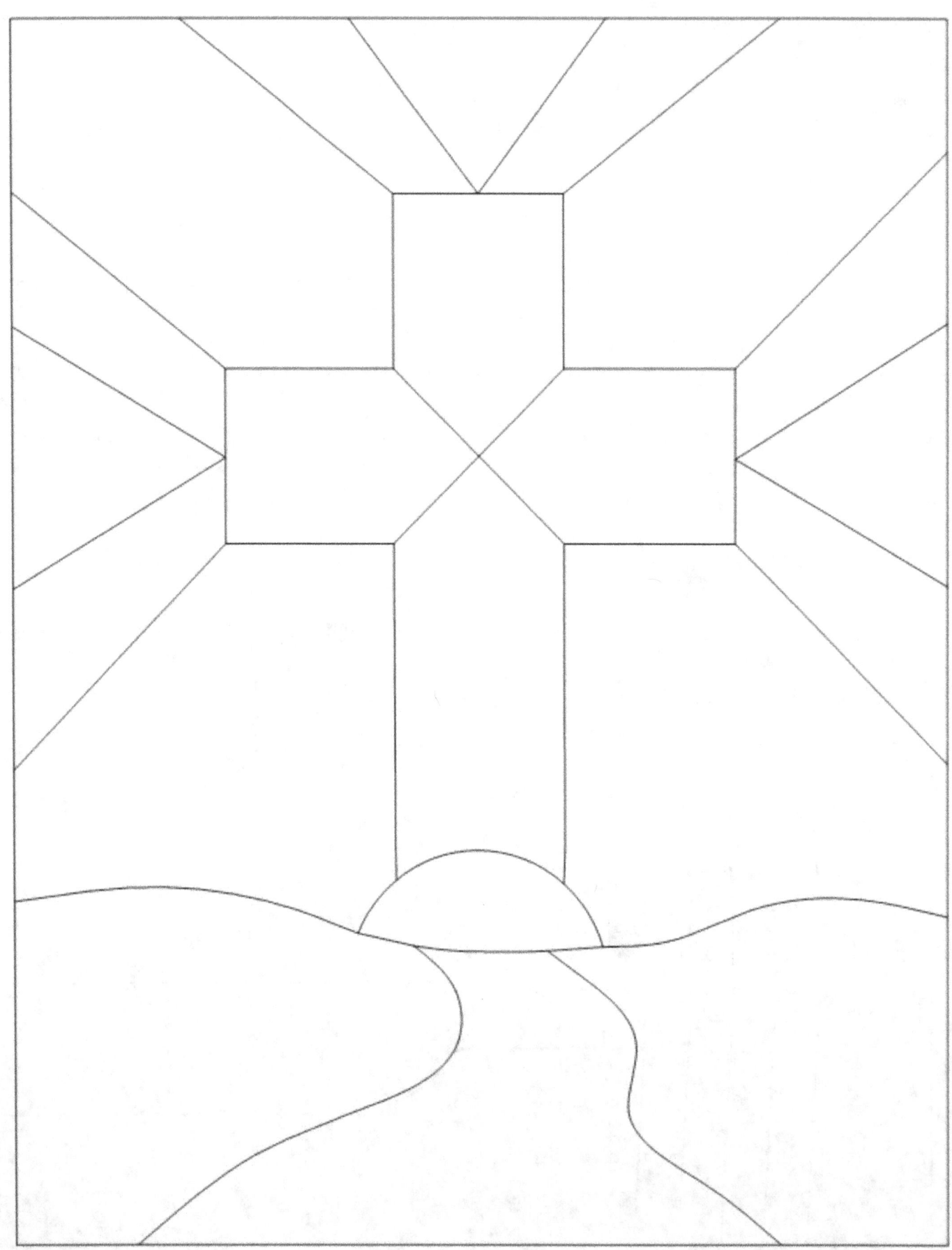

#32 Heart Cross

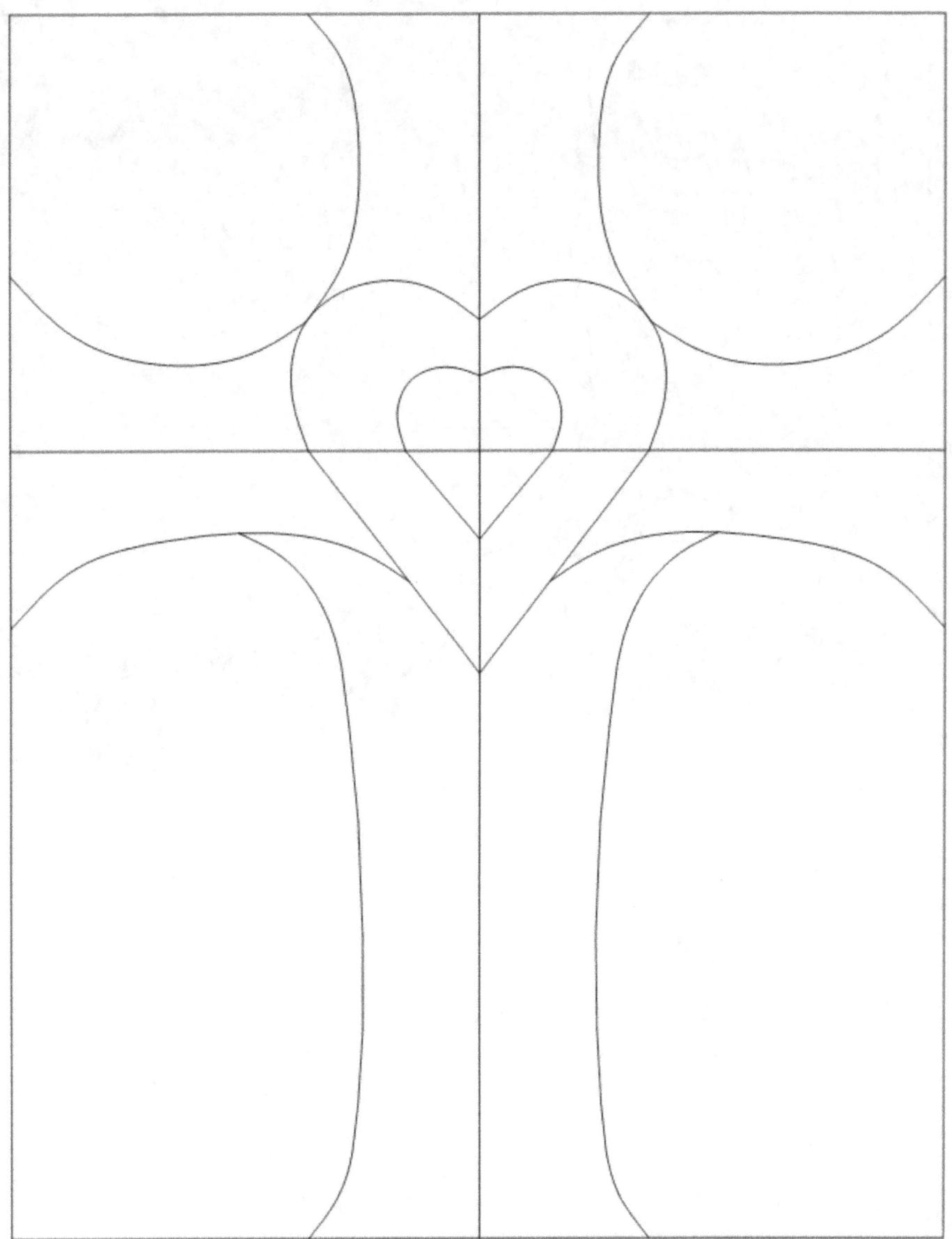

#33 Jesus' Tomb

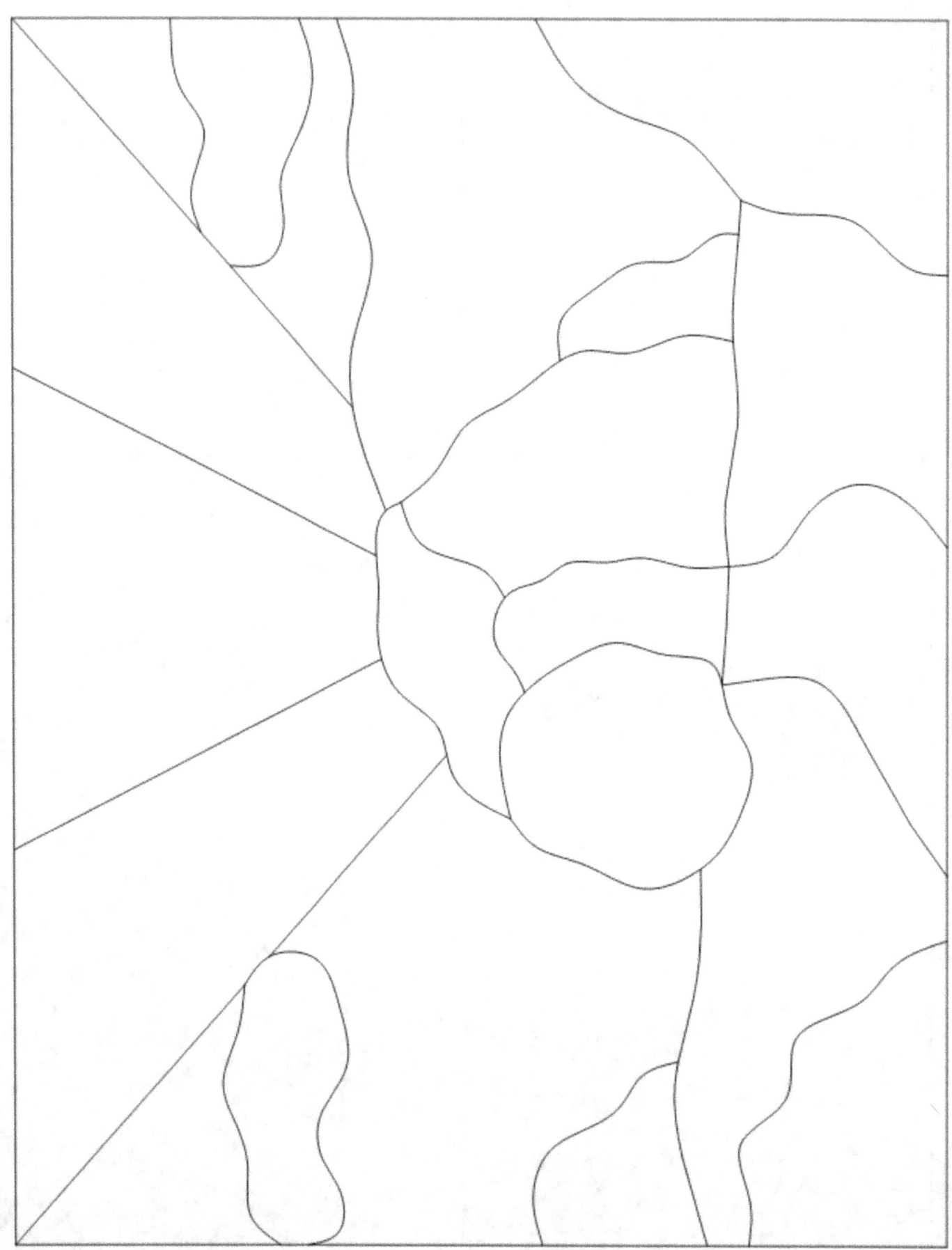

#34 Carrying of the Cross

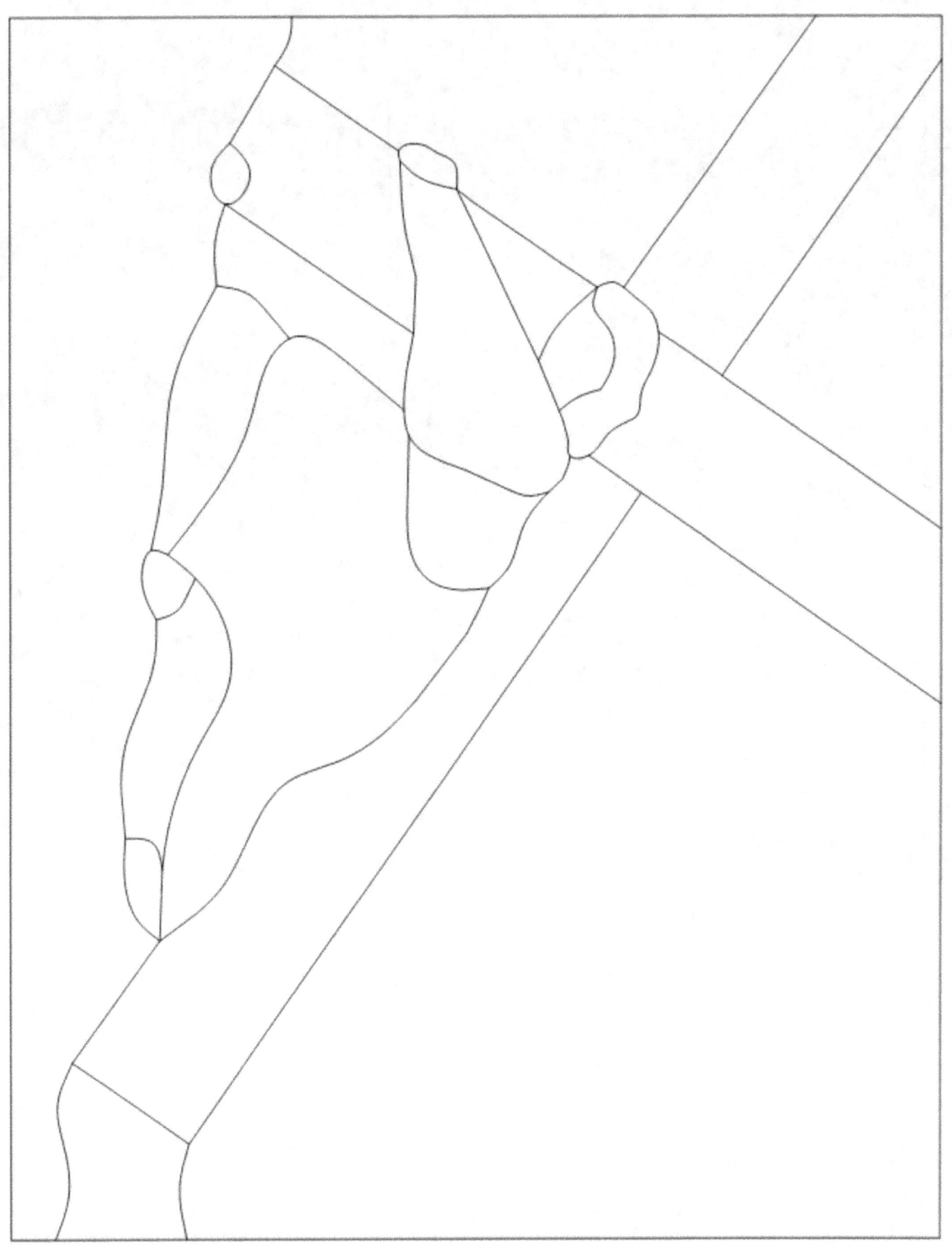

#35 Praying

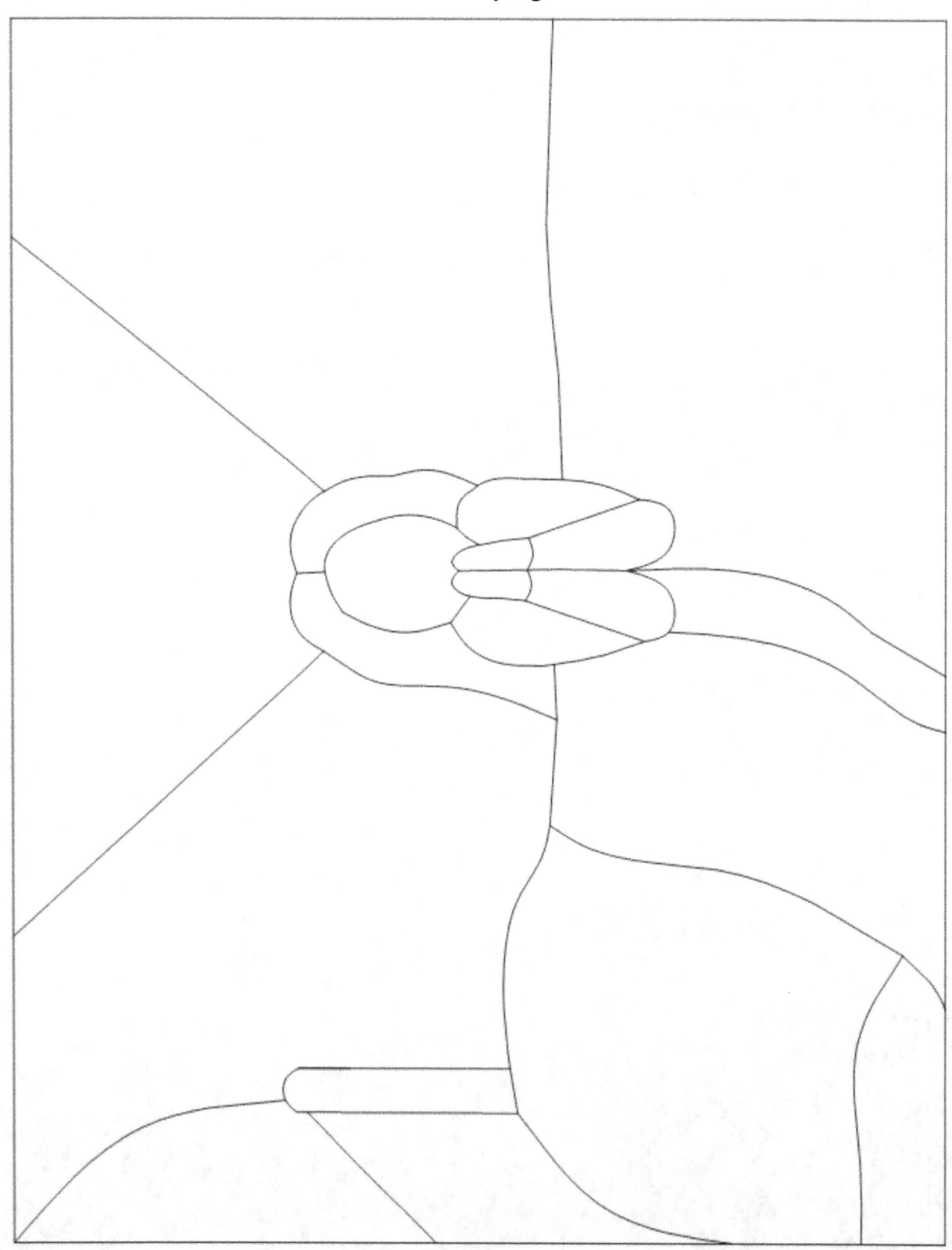

Acknowledgements

I owe many thanks to different people for the success of this book.

To those who bought this book and want to spread the Signs of God, please continue spreading the Word of God through everything you do and say.

To my wife, Cassandra Hennigan-Williams, for her continued support and encouragement to continue doing something I love.

To my father and mother, Paul G. and Ann M. Williams, whose love and guidance have kept my artistic endeavors alive all these years.

To my sister, Pam, who has always told me that I am better and smarter than I ever think I am.

To my good friend, Kelly Hoium, who is my editor and a very patient person.

To my mentor, Jacqui Bush, from Stained Glass of McKinney, for introducing me to the world of stained glass and giving me the guidance and the leadership to fuel this project.

Stained Glass of McKinney, 214 N. Kentucky Street, McKinney, TX 75069 (Art Glass Association's 2010 Retailer of the Year Award.)

To the rest of my family and friends, my sincere thanks.

Most of all, and above all, I want to thank Our Lord Jesus Christ, for without Him none of this would have ever been possible!

Thank You and God Bless!

James A. Williams

www.ingramcontent.com/pod-product-compliance
Lightning Source LLC
Chambersburg PA
CBHW081239170526
45165CB00009B/3119